WILD HEART

The Story of
JOY ADAMSON,
Author of *Born Free*

Anne E. Neimark

Harcourt Brace & Company

San Diego   New York   London

Though a small portion of dialogue in this biography of
Joy Adamson is fictionalized, most was found among her
writings. Perhaps as convincing a record are Joy's
photographs—some of which are presented in
this book. They tell a wondrous story of their own.

Photographs reprinted by permission of the
Elsa Conservation Trust.

Epigraph from *The Philosophy of Civilization* by Albert Schweitzer
(Amherst, NY: Prometheus Books). Copyright 1988.
Reprinted by permission of the publisher.

Library of Congress Cataloging-in-Publication Data
Neimark, Anne E.
Wild heart: the story of Joy Adamson, author of *Born Free/*
by Anne E. Neimark.
p. cm.
Includes bibliographical references.
Summary: Discusses the life and work of the woman
best known for her relationship with a lion cub,
described in her book *Born Free*.
ISBN 0-15-201368-7
1. Adamson, Joy—Juvenile literature. 2. Zoologists—Kenya—Biography—
Juvenile literature. 3. Wildlife conservationists—Kenya—Biography—
Juvenile literature. [1. Adamson, Joy. 2. Zoologists.
3. Women—Biography.] I. Title.
QL31.A33N45 1999
590'.92—dc21
[B]   98-26097

Text set in Bembo
Designed by Lydia D'moch
First edition
A C E F D B
Printed in the United States of America

To Chet—
who teaches me to welcome the light

"Until he extends the circle of his compassion
to all living things, man will not himself find peace."

—*Albert Schweitzer*

$\mathcal{I}$NTRODUCTION

JOY ADAMSON was a pioneer in two worlds: one, the rewarding but often perilous world of wild animal research; the other, the world of art in service to science. Rescuing, sheltering, and studying hundreds of animals and birds in Kenya, Africa—where, from 1937 to 1980, she lived a rugged safari life—Joy brought new and exciting knowledge to ethology (the science of animal behavior). She showed, for example, that animals are far more intelligent and emotionally developed than had been believed, and she demonstrated that they can communicate with one another over many miles.

Scientists had thought that once a wild animal had been domesticated, it could not survive in the wild. Joy proved them wrong. Her pioneering return of a domesticated lion, cheetah, and leopard to freedom was historic. She wrote best-selling books about a variety of animals and raised money for national parks and reserves in both the United States and Europe. She used her own funds to help establish four national parks in Kenya (Meru, Shaba, Samburu, and Hell's Gate) and to support animal orphanages, sanctuaries, and welfare organizations. Her efforts led to what are now called the Green movements, which work to save endangered species, raise the world's consciousness about humane treatment of animals, and protect the environment from pollution.

Joy had an extraordinary bond with Elsa, the beloved lion of her world-famous *Born Free* book trilogy and the Oscar-winning movie *Born Free,* changing the way the world understands and treats wild and domestic animals. Joy adored Elsa as if she were her own child, but—with unprecedented skill—she bravely and successfully returned Elsa to her natural habitat.

Joy's second world of achievement lay in painting and drawing. Her work hangs in museums, galleries, and private collections around the world. Her detailed paintings, praised by scientists, often show formerly unknown species of fish and reptiles she encountered on her travels in Africa. Her hundreds of paintings of members from more than forty native tribes of Kenya (some hang in the State House there) provide a valuable look at what has disappeared in the march of civilization—the bold, colorful costumes and rituals of Africa's native population.

Joy grew up in Silesia, an area of Austria that, after World War I, became part of Czechoslovakia. The name given her at birth was Friederike Victoria Gessner. Not until she was twenty-eight did she agree to be called Joy—at the request of her second husband. Little did she know then that her final name of Joy Adamson, recorded at her third marriage, would become so well-known and respected. Even though Joy chose to leave her childhood home at Seifenmühle, the glamorous Austrian estate of her maternal grandmother, for the dangers, the challenges, and the animals of Africa, she was always influenced by the deep pleasures and sorrows of her early years. She paid attention, however, to her maternal great-grandfather's words. He was a man who, though opposed and even ridiculed, built the first successful water turbine to provide electrical power in Czechoslovakia. "If something needs to be done," her great-grandfather told her, "do it *now*."

After she had achieved fame, Joy went on two world tours that took her back to see friends and family in Europe. Although her Austrian accent made her nervous about speaking in public, especially in the United States, she gave lectures, held press conferences, even spoke at a London prison. Her tours brought her the exposure she needed to keep her books and articles selling, to find homes for her extraordinary photographs of animals, and to raise money for her causes. She was awarded, in 1977, the Austrian Cross of Honor for Science and Arts, the highest tribute of its kind that her homeland could bestow.

Joy's adventures in Africa were breathtaking and suspenseful. She went on camel, donkey, car, and walking safaris; climbed mountains where the air was so thin she could hardly breathe; endured scorching heat, freezing temperatures, and raging winds; and was beset by floods that sometimes destroyed her makeshift camps. She was chased by buffalo, elephants, lions, and rhinos. She rescued big animals like elephants, and tiny birds like weavers. She never stopped loving Africa and was amazingly energetic, creative, and emotional. Joy Adamson was as much a wild heart as any animal who came into her care.

CHAPTER 1

CROUCHED BENEATH a thick spray of willow branches, the girl was silent. Slivers of sun pressing through the leaves streaked her blond hair almost white; wildflowers nestled like tiny wings against her legs. In the distance, Friederike could hear her friends and cousins yelling— "We'll find you, Friederike!"—as they raced over the grounds at Seifenmühle, the Austrian estate owned by her grandmother. Swimming pool, tennis courts, boats, and horses were ignored in the frenzy of Lion Hunt, a favorite game of the dozen or so children.

Friederike and her cousin Peter were always chosen to be lions. Seifenmühle was so huge that the "hunters" sometimes had to stalk their "prey" for hours. By suppertime, if both lions were caught, the hunters won the game—and the "kingdom."

As she hid, Friederike plucked auricula blossoms from the ground under the willow tree. How she loved flowers! Her favorite birthday present had been a flowering plant for her room, which she regretted leaving each morning when she went to school.

The shouts of the hunters grew closer, and Friederike dropped to her knees. She barely allowed herself a breath. It was always hard for her to stay still; her father called her unruly. Maybe, she thought, that was why she was such a good lion in the game. She ran faster than her friends; she climbed trees in a flash; she refused to cry if she was hurt. And, like a yellow mane, her hair would fly out in the wind.

When she was born, on January 20, 1910, her father had been angry she wasn't a boy. His name for her was Fritz; he treated her like a boy and wanted her to wear long pants.

It was her mother, beautiful and stylish, who bought her ruffled dresses. Her mother could sing and paint—"a voice and hand from heaven," said Milli, the cook. At age ten, Friederike hungered for her mother to favor her over her two sisters, twelve-year-old Traute and two-year-old Dorle. Friederike once left a poem under her mother's pillow, a private declaration of love, but her mother showed the poem to casual friends. Hurt, Friederike then tore up some of her other poetry.

The hunters had passed by. Reaching for a thick tree limb above her, Friederike stealthily pulled herself upward and straddled the trunk. Willow branches covered her in green cascades. In two weeks, she reminded herself, there would be more children at Seifenmühle, all staying in the main villa. Cousins would arrive, not only from Austria but also from Italy, Germany, England, and America. They would be greeted by an inscription on the villa door:

Ten were invited, twenty have come,
Put water in the soup and make them welcome.

At the swimming pool, Friederike always raced her cousins on bicycles down a wooden rail from the diving board into the water. Visitors and family competed in high jumping, target shooting, and discus throwing—and in the evenings, they dressed in costumes to present plays or sing to the music of the "Seifenmühle Cousins' Band." At summer's end, peasant workers arrived at Seifenmühle for the harvest festival, its highlight a party with cakes, cookies, and fruit juice in the barn.

One of Friederike's cousins, heat reddening her face, suddenly darted under the willow branches, but she didn't see the motionless form on the limb. "We've caught Peter!" the cousin shouted. "We found him in a barrel! Where are you, O Great Lioness?"

The faint ringing of the supper bell told Friederike that Lion Hunt was over. With only Peter captured, the hunters could not claim the kingdom. Friederike jumped down from the willow tree, ripping her shorts on a branch, and ran triumphantly toward the villa.

Dinner guests would soon arrive for the annual postwar concert of band music. Two years earlier, when Friederike was eight, World War I had ended, toppling the Austro-Hungarian Empire and making the region of

Silesia, where Seifenmühle lay, a part of the new Czechoslovakia.

The war was still a constant topic among the adults at Seifenmühle. Friederike's maternal grandmother, Oma, lived in Vienna, the once glamorous capital of the Austro-Hungarian Empire; now the city seemed cast adrift, its economy and pride devastated. Yet for Friederike, World War I had brought a new activity to Seifenmühle: Bank notes recycled in her great-grandfather's paper factories had become so inflated in value that, after the armistice, a trillion-mark note was needed to buy a dozen eggs. Because paper itself was still valuable, the notes were stored inside huge silos where Friederike and her friends made tunnels, playing among billions of certificates.

At the villa Friederike saw her father, Viktor Gessner, waiting at the front door. Above him, like welcoming arms, small-paned windows were flung open. Viktor Gessner, however, was scowling. "You're late, Fritz!" he barked at his daughter. "Guests are coming. And look at you—you're filthy! Twigs in your hair and your shorts torn! Come here!"

Standing beside her father, Friederike watched four men approaching. "You will be introduced," her father said, "though you're a shameful sight. And you will be polite. These men were under my command in our motorized unit during the war."

Viktor Gessner seized his daughter's hand and yanked her closer. While he greeted the men his hand closed around her fingers like iron bars of a cage, squeezing down with such force that Friederike's knuckles felt as if they were on fire. Gasping slightly, she tried to pull away, but her hand was trapped in the viselike grip of her father's anger. She thought of the animal traps on Seifenmühle's grounds; she could almost hear the heart-searing sounds of dying rabbits, roebucks, foxes, and deer.

Friederike managed a curtsy as she was introduced to the guests. Peter, her other cousins, and her friends would applaud her, she reminded herself. She—the Great Lioness—had not been captured today; she was too strong and clever. Whenever she chose, she could be Queen of the Brave Beasts of Seifenmühle.

Friederike lifted her chin and took a deep breath. She would not, she told herself, give in to cowardice. And even while her hand continued to sting under the punishing grip of her father, she knew that she would not cry.

AT THE AGE of eighty-two, Friederike's great-grandfather died. He had been bruised and shaken when, driving to inspect a forest, his sleigh had turned over and slid down a slope. Undaunted, he'd gone on to see the forest; at lunch he'd developed a mild headache. Later he was found dead in his bed.

Friederike watched the funeral from one of the villa's second-floor windows. Sadly, yet proudly, she saw there were hundreds of mourners in the procession led by the local fire department band. The large crowd included the peasants who worked at Seifenmühle, some paper factory employees, most of the nearby villagers, and adult family and friends.

Losing her great-grandfather was painful for Friederike. He'd always had time for her. Her parents often seemed distracted, and her grandmother Oma was still in Vienna. Now she would have only two grown-up companions—Orga, the Hungarian coachman who had a stiff leg but took her mushroom hunting, and Milli, the cook.

Friederike loved to hear Milli's wonderful stories. But the cook was no pushover. If Friederike acted up, Milli called for a slimy creature named Bubutz. Though Friederike believed Bubutz was imaginary, she wasn't quite sure. "Milli's Bubutz," her mother told her, "is all that ever scares you!"

Whenever Friederike awakened from bad dreams, she thought of Bubutz. Then, no matter what time of day or night, she would want to water her flowering plant, or smell cut violets, or hear Chopin played on the piano.

Animals soothed her, also. During the war she'd had a pet rabbit named Hasi—a soft albino with a fluffy tail. Friederike would sit with Hasi on her lap, stroking his fur and letting him eat from her hand. He'd rub his nose on her fingers and make tiny noises. One evening, however, as the family encircled the supper table, rabbit stew was served. When everyone said how good it tasted, Friederike's mother remarked that the stew was Hasi. Friederike fled the table and hid in the back of her closet.

Although hunting and killing animals was common at Seifenmühle, Friederike hated the organized kills in which beaters drove a terrified animal into a circle of hunters aiming their guns. And outside the kitchen, she always stopped to speak softly to the weasel-like marten who was kept in a cage to amuse the children. The little animal could barely turn around in its wire prison.

One afternoon Friederike went with Seifenmühle's gamekeeper on his daily rounds. Having hiked past six deer and three gray partridges with brown markings, they were resting on a tree stump when a roebuck, or male roe deer, loped to the edge of a pond. After it drank, the roebuck turned toward Friederike and the gamekeeper, the late-afternoon sun haloing its body in a bronze glow.

"Here," said the gamekeeper to Friederike, "take my rifle."

"But why?" Friederike asked.

"The roebuck's antlers are malformed. I want you to kill it."

"No!" Friederike blurted out. "I can't! I won't!"

"Look, missy," the gamekeeper said, "someone has to shoot this roebuck. It's defective. You're growing up, aren't you? You're not a weakling, are you? In town, they say you're as brave as a boy. Show me."

Confused, her heart thumping, Friederike stood up and slowly took the rifle. She remembered her great-grandfather saying, "If something must be done, do it now"—but was this something that *must* be done? Did the gamekeeper know best? Did it matter if antlers were malformed?

Dizzy, her arms shaking, Friederike raised the rifle, aiming it as she'd been taught. Through the rifle sight, she glimpsed the calm but questioning gaze of the roebuck, the length of its neck, the brown bulge of its chest. Her thoughts tumbled in disarray as she squeezed on the cold curve of the trigger. Sound burst in her ears. Stiffly the roebuck rose, shuddering, before it fell to the ground.

What have I done? Friederike asked herself in despair. *Aren't I a friend to the animals here? Didn't the roebuck deserve to live, as my Hasi deserved to live?*

The gamekeeper, having found a pole on which to string up the roebuck, smiled broadly at Friederike. "Good job, missy!" he said. "Here, I'll put this pine twig in your buttonhole. It's dipped in the roebuck's blood. Everyone at the villa will know you're a true hunter."

Sneaking away later from the supper table, a sour ache in her stomach, Friederike walked with her cousin Peter to their favorite meadow, fireflies and stars twinkling above them. "I feel like a murderer," Friederike said softly.

"Sometimes," Peter told her, flopping down on his stomach, "animals have to be killed. Sometimes Lion Hunt is more than a game."

"I want you to hear my vow," Friederike announced suddenly. "I will never shoot an animal for sport. I'll spend part of my life studying animals! I'll travel far away to discover new animals! Do you believe me, Peter? Tell me you believe me."

"Oh yes," Peter answered her, his narrow face tilted toward the stars hanging in a canopy over Seifenmühle's meadow. "Whatever you say you'll do, Friederike, I believe it. Nothing in all the world will ever stop you."

CHAPTER 2

AS POSTWAR EUROPE struggled to repair its bombed-out cities, wounds appeared that did not heal. The armistice had put Silesia, where Seifenmühle lay, within Czechoslovakia's borders. Friederike now studied the Czech language, but she clung to speaking German and insisted she was still Austrian.

Friederike's new nationality was not the only painful change in her life. In spring of 1922 her parents suddenly divorced. Her mother, weary of the dark soberness in Viktor Gessner, had fallen in love with Hans Hofmann, a tutor at Seifenmühle. She soon remarried, fired Milli the cook, and left the care of her children to governesses.

Friederike felt a burning inside her when she thought of her parents' divorce. Had she ever, she wondered, been what they wanted? She wasn't a boy for her father; she had never been certain of her mother's devotion. Now the divorce had stolen any chance for a safe, loving family. Only her grandmother seemed aware that beneath Friederike's flashing eyes and defiant tilt of chin there was sorrow. Warm and sympathetic, Oma cooked elaborate suppers for Friederike, encouraging her to invite friends to the table. "Your wings are meant to fly," Oma said.

"I told Peter," Friederike answered, leaning against her grandmother's arm, "that someday I'll go far away. Animals will live with me—and I won't abandon them."

AT AGE THIRTEEN Friederike began attending boarding school. She earned high marks in her studies and participated in many activities. She was asked to paint a mural of a village band on a dormitory wall, and she acted in French and English plays. A music professor from Salzburg was engaged to teach her the piano.

When her mother visited the school, Friederike was grateful not to be sharing her with Hans Hofmann. At holidays, however, Friederike had to deal with her stepfather, who was known in Europe as an anti-Semite, an enemy of the Jewish population. Friederike tried to be gracious to him, especially at Christmas; but eventually, because Hans made nasty remarks about her Jewish school friends, she refused to see her mother unless he was away.

In 1925 Friederike announced she would leave boarding school to focus on piano. She and her sister Traute were sent to Vienna to live with Oma, and seven-year-old Dorle went to Troppau with their father. For two years Friederike trained for the state piano certificate, which would allow her to teach. She took classes in harmony, composition, and counterpoint, and practiced so hard that she strained both hands. "It is not just over-work," an instructor told her. "Such small hands as yours will suffer and fail you on octaves. Certainly you can teach piano, but you cannot have a career as a professional pianist."

"I love the piano," Friederike answered, "and I want to learn as many of the arts as possible. But I haven't settled on a career."

Piano practice helped keep Friederike from dwelling on loss or disappointment. When she heard that her father had remarried, she played Mozart and Chopin long into the night. Even though she had not seen Dorle for months, she would not visit her younger sister alongside her father and his new wife. She did not see very much of either parent. Both, she felt, had betrayed her.

After her seventeenth birthday, Friederike received notice of the examination for her piano certificate. Her heart sank when she read the program she would play. Most of the compositions and scales she could handle with ease, but the last piece, by Alfred Reynolds, included long series of octaves. Whenever she practiced Reynolds, her hands cramped. No matter how much she warmed up, she would feel the ninth or tenth octave stiffen her fingers.

The morning of the examination, Friederike was slicing Danish bread in Oma's kitchen. The knife slipped suddenly and plunged into her left thumb. Blood spurted onto the counter. Friederike bent awkwardly over her injury and pressed down on the cut with her right hand.

How, she asked herself, could she perform at the examination? Escaping from bread, knife, and blood, she ran to the bathroom to find a box of gauze. As she wiped her thumb on a towel and bandaged the wound, she reminded herself that if she missed the examination, she would have to wait another year. "I *must* play," she whispered to her ashen face in the mirror.

At the examination hall she took her place with other students in a row of high-backed chairs as one by one the applicants were tested. After more than an hour her name was called. The examiner appeared startled when he saw her bandage, but he smiled sympathetically as Friederike walked toward the piano.

Her hands rested lightly on the keyboard, her left thumb an odd-looking knob of white cotton. She played scales, hoping she could hit the proper keys in perfect order. When she'd finished the exercise, she kept her head lowered, looking neither right nor left, and began selections by Bach and Beethoven. Music poured from the piano, tone and tempo in a lilting blend. Raising her head to glance at the examiner, Friederike saw him still smiling.

Then it was time for Reynolds. Lifting her hands from her lap, she started to play with fierce resolve. If only her fingers could stretch to the impossible octaves, she told herself. Instead, no more than thirty seconds into the piece, she watched in alarm as the gauze on her thumb split and blood covered the keys.

"Stop!" the examiner bellowed. "Enough! Please find a cloth for the young lady."

Friederike was handed a handkerchief, which she twisted around her thumb. Expecting to be disqualified from the exam, she rose from the piano bench, trying to accept the inevitable postponement of her certificate. But just as two ladies came to clean the keys and Friederike was making her exit through double doors, she heard the examiner call: "Friederike Viktoria Gessner."

She paused in midflight, like a startled bird. "You performed with great excellence," the examiner said. "You have met the requirements for your certificate. I will not expect you to repeat the Reynolds."

Friederike could hardly believe her good luck. If her bandage had not broken, she thought with delight, she probably would have failed the exam. Someone must have been looking out for her—someone other than her mother or father, other even than Oma—some presence, she assured herself as she dashed from the hall, who had heard all of her secret dreams without turning away.

HER STATE CERTIFICATE in hand, Friederike could accept piano students, but the part of her that her father had called unruly wanted more than teaching. If she had gained one skill, earned one certificate, why not others? She enrolled in dressmaking school, where, in two years, she would acquire the Gremium diploma; at night she took singing lessons, learned how to restore old pictures, drew posters and book jackets, and studied typing and shorthand. When Peter visited Vienna, he sat with her at an outdoor café. "I'm moving to Canada," he said. "You could come with me."

She slowly shook her head. "I want to stay here," she answered, "and try to combine what I love—art, music, nature. I don't know my exact direction, but I hope to live among animals. That I do know."

"Beauty and the beasts," Peter remarked softly.

In the summer Friederike returned to Seifenmühle. Even there, however, she was restless, hiking for hours. When she heard that a sculptor named Kapps lived nearby, she talked Oma into letting her study with him. Kapps was creating a war memorial, a gigantic copper figure of Jesus Christ. The metalwork intrigued Friederike, and she learned to emboss silver plates, also encrusting them with colorful stones. From wood, she carved a woman holding a rabbit and wondered afterward if she had memorialized Hasi.

The apprenticeship with Kapps ended when Friederike saw she was more than student to him. Kapps's marriage was failing, and he threw himself into painting Friederike's portrait, staring at her through slitted eyes as she posed. Suddenly, though he knew his proposal was improper, he asked her to pose in the nude. Friederike hastily departed for Vienna. She was eighteen now, slim and shapely, she realized as she glimpsed her reflection in a train window. Men gaped at her in stores, yet she did not see herself as a grown woman. She'd watched animals mating, but sexual matters had never been explained to her, and she felt ignorant on the subject.

That winter Oma sent Friederike on skiing holidays to meet eligible men. She did meet a Hungarian who, smitten with her, asked her to marry him. Though she was flattered, she refused, and returned from the holiday uncommitted.

Oma soon arranged for Friederike to take dancing lessons so she could attend the Hofburg ball in Vienna's imperial castle. The night of the ball, Friederike combed her hair around her ears and excitedly rouged her cheeks. But the occasion proved disappointing. Waltzing along with other guests at the debutante ball, she winced as her partners clumsily stepped on her toes.

Though she had tried, with encouragement from her sister Traute, to repair relations with her mother (whose name also was Traute), Friederike resented her mother's insistent questions about her father. Yes, she answered her mother, she occasionally exchanged letters with him. No, she still was not comfortable with her stepfather. When her mother criticized Viktor Gessner, Friederike withdrew. Soon she stopped visiting.

One morning not long after the younger Traute married, Friederike received a telephone call from her mother. "Your father has died," her mother said. "An autopsy showed an unknown disease of the spleen. Doctors are pleased over the new findings. Your father's spleen is on exhibit at the Prague Medical Museum."

Friederike had barely hung up the phone when, stunned by her mother's announcement, she fell dizzily to the floor. She managed to pull herself into a chair, sitting rigidly until she could rise to her feet and leave the house. Outside, she plucked a pink wildflower growing between cobblestones, rubbing its petals against her mouth.

When she told her grandmother the news, Friederike was wearing a gold brooch Oma had given her, a carving of the goddess Diana wearing the Order of the Golden Fleece, the highest European order of chivalry. "Darling," Oma had said, "I wish the brooch to bring you strength."

THROUGH ALL OF Friederike's restlessness—through the myriad lessons, classes, and certificates, through the shock of the Gessner divorce—Oma had seemed to trust her granddaughter's choices. She gave Friederike permission to attend the Gschnas, the grand ball of Vienna's art world, even though Friederike planned to appear without an escort. Unlike the Hofburg ball, the Gschnas was considered daring and eccentric. A friend redesigned Friederike's white satin Hofburg gown, cutting away half the skirt so that one leg would show. Over the dress and onto her skin, Friederike painted a bold pattern with greasepaint. Oma gasped at the sight of her but did not withdraw her permission.

At the Künstlerhaus, the dignified building given over each year to the Gschnas, provocative murals had been painted on the walls. Bright lights, loud music, and garish costumes set up a carnival atmosphere. Friederike—hoping now, like Oma, that she might meet an eligible young man—was startled by such arty sophistication. She felt unsure among the costumed strangers, their drinks spilling heedlessly on each other, their mouths often smirking or grim. "I'll take a quick look," she murmured to herself, "and then go home."

Minutes later, wedged in among three dark-haired women with long-lashed, sensual eyes and fingernails like stilettos, Friederike pushed herself forward. One of the women bent down to scrape a fingernail along Friederike's bare leg. "Why not rip off the rest of your skirt?" the woman rasped. The Gschnas, Friederike realized, was more brazen than she'd imagined. Wild animals might be tame in comparison. Parties and festivals at Seifenmühle, where she'd spent so many hours, had never been tawdry or vulgar.

Just then, as Friederike bolted away from the woman with the probing fingernail, someone seized her by the shoulders, spinning her around. She found herself held by a tall masked man, a guest who was dressed as a French apache, or ruffian. "You are *mine*," the man said, picking her up and carrying her off. She felt the strength of his arms and the gritty warmth of his body. Mute, she tried to see his eyes behind the holes in the mask. What she could not know at that moment was that this unknown "apache" was carrying her on a romantic journey far greater than the width of the Künstlerhaus dance hall— a journey that, in the next several weeks, would take her from girlhood into womanhood.

CHAPTER 3

THE AFFAIR lasted two years. Friederike and her apache traveled across Europe, drinking in history and culture. In Italy, they drove through the Dolomite Alps, veering southward to Florence and the Tuscan countryside, then visiting Milan's art galleries, museums, and cathedrals. In Switzerland, they hiked to the hut where the artist Giovanni Segantini had painted, and to the glacier that had inspired Nietzsche, the German philosopher, to write *Thus Spake Zarathustra*.

The relationship eventually ended, according to a friend, when Friederike became pregnant—though she never admitted her condition publicly. Her suitor refused to marry her and emigrated to America. Friederike did not want to shame her family; with great trepidation and guilt, she had an illegal abortion. Afterward, dangerously ill, she slowly recovered but felt betrayed and abandoned—again. Her apache, she wrote later, had "aroused emotions sometimes almost beyond what I could bear."

All that remained to her was Plinkus, a tiny dachshund he'd given her.

Depressed and withdrawn, Friederike was urged by several friends to consult a doctor trained in psychoanalysis, the method of exploring the unconscious mind for repressed feelings that can cause emotional and physical illness. Sigmund Freud, creator of psychoanalysis, lived in Vienna; his "talking cure" was the latest fashion across the city. For a year Friederike spent five hours a week with a psychoanalyst. Then, feeling stronger, she began to study sculpture with Professor Wilhelm Frass, whose studio was on a tree-lined stretch of land along the river Danube.

From Frass, Friederike learned advanced techniques of sculpting in stone, marble, wood, wax, and clay. One of her creations was a standing girl whose head was turned aside, hidden by raised arms. Some of Friederike's sadness seemed to be transferred onto the figure.

Moments of tranquillity came when she walked in the woods with Plinkus, or, in the winter, when she skied. She looked to nature to calm her, and she was eager to escape the round of social events in Vienna. Yet, at the age of twenty-three, she still had not found her "purpose." An interest in Indonesian carving almost took her to Bali and the Solomon Islands, but she soon dropped the idea. Medical student friends allowed her into a hospital dissecting room, where she was so struck by human anatomy that she actually signed up for a medical program at the university. But she was bored by chemistry, mathematics, and physics.

"All my girlfriends are either married or working," she'd say to Oma. "You've been so patient with me. I know I'm a financial burden."

"Hush," Oma would tell her. "Your day will come. You're never a burden."

One skiing weekend, as Friederike zigzagged down a steep, snowy slope, a man skied beside her. When they both came to a halt, the man took off his knit cap and held out his hand. "I'm Viktor von Klarwill," he said, "but my friends call me Ziebel. I'm so pleased to meet you. I've watched you from afar."

By sundown, Friederike and Ziebel were still on the slope, exchanging stories. Ziebel was a successful Austrian car dealer with a yen to leave his city job to live "the natural life." He was fascinated by birds and he loved music and travel. Friederike thought she had met a kindred spirit. For three weeks they saw each other every day. During the fourth week Ziebel asked Friederike to drop her studies and marry him, promising her that, with Plinkus, they'd find a home somewhere and be happy.

On July 28, 1935, with only local witnesses attending, Friederike and Ziebel were married in Ramsau, a resort southeast of Salzburg. They traveled all summer in Europe, and when winter arrived, went back to the ski slopes. Though he was more easygoing than his new wife, Ziebel doted on Friederike.

Their courtship, however, had been too brief to build a solid foundation for marriage. Their opinions often matched, but their personalities greatly differed. "We'll settle in some other country," Ziebel said, "and our true life will begin."

Friederike and Ziebel both investigated the possibility of emigrating to Tahiti, Tasmania, or California. They also contacted a Swiss farmer in Kenya, Africa. Uncertain of a permanent destination, they traveled through France, visiting Avignon, Carcassonne, Chartres, and Paris, then went on to Belgium and Holland. By the spring of 1937, war rumors and the sword of German nationalism hovered over Central Europe. Happily, Friederike learned she was pregnant, but she ignored her doctor's advice and went skiing near Siefenmühle.

"Be careful," Ziebel warned.

"I'll be fine," she answered. But she was not. After several days on the slopes, she suffered a miscarriage. She grew silent and remote, and to add to her sorrow, Plinkus suddenly died. "You need to get away from Vienna," Ziebel told her.

It was decided she would take a boat from the port of Genoa, Italy, to Mombasa, Africa. She would stay with the Swiss farmer in Kenya, recuperate from her miscarriage, and look for a farm where she and Ziebel might live. Ziebel would follow when he could leave Austria unnoticed; half-Jewish, he was under scrutiny by Germany's Nazi regime, which was spreading anti-Semitic hatred and monitoring travel. No one but Oma was told of the plans.

Near Genoa, Friederike and Ziebel stayed briefly with friends who kept praising a local fortune-teller. In curiosity, Friederike scribbled two questions on paper for the man. Would she continue living in Vienna, she asked, and would she bear children? "I did not sign the paper," she said later, "or give my address, but placed it in a sealed envelope and asked my friends to keep the reply until I called for it."

On May 12, 1937, Friederike boarded the ship for Africa. Her heart was racing from last-minute anxiety and some misgivings. What would she *really* feel, alone in a country unknown to her? What dangers might lie ahead? Did the fortune-teller know? Ziebel had embraced her, assuring her that the future would shine on them, but as Friederike waved to him from the ship railing, she felt cast adrift and unsure.

AT THE Suez Canal, Friederike and a group of other passengers took a side trip to Cairo, Egypt. They toured the Cairo museum, Friederike staying behind to linger over the exhibit of artifacts from the reign of Egyptian pharaoh Tutankhamen. In the afternoon she and the group rode camels at the Giza pyramids and tracked coral fish at the Red Sea.

Reboarding the ship, Friederike found a new passenger on deck, a dark-haired man who introduced himself as Peter Bally. Born in Switzerland, Peter, a chemist, had worked in India and Africa but had recently turned to botany and was completing a book on medicinal plants. He invited Friederike to a game of table tennis, charming her by talking to the ball in German, English, and Swahili, the major language of Africa. Friederike joined him for dinner, twisting her wedding ring on her finger and wondering why it seemed that she and this man she'd just met were old and true friends.

"My husband," she told Peter, "is waiting to hear if I like Africa enough to live there with him."

By the time the ship reached Mombasa, the largest port in East Africa, Friederike knew that she'd fallen in love with forty-three-year-old Peter Bally. Despair had swung to hope inside her—as if Ziebel were tied to the darkness of the miscarriage, and Peter, who was in the process of divorce, was the African sun. From Mombasa Peter went on to Nairobi, capital of Kenya, and Friederike traveled on to the farmer in Kitale. For a week she tried to escape her feelings, but it was, she would say, "a hopeless struggle." Peter visited her at the farm, also feeling conflicted. He convinced her to return to Austria to give her marriage another try.

Once again Friederike boarded ship, this time to return to Vienna. When she confessed the situation to Ziebel, he was despondent. A reconciliation was attempted, but it failed over a few months. Ziebel sadly agreed to a divorce. Friederike wrote Peter a letter, booked passage back to Africa, and while waiting for departure day, went to her friends' home near Genoa to retrieve the fortune-teller's predictions. *You will live in the tropics*, the fortune-teller had said. *You will need to learn English. You will never have children.*

In March 1938, on the day before the Nazis marched into Vienna and one year before much of the world declared war on Germany, Friederike said good-bye to Oma and began the journey to Africa. In spite of the fortune-teller's words, she'd sewn some dresses that could be "let out" if she became pregnant.

She had hardly any money, she was leaving her homeland behind her, and she knew little of the English she'd need for talking to Caucasians in Africa. When she arrived in Nairobi, she heard with relief that Peter had been appointed botanist at the city's Coryndon (now Nairobi) Museum. He and she would have a good reason to live in this land that burst out before her in rocky hills, volcanoes, and deserts, in wetlands and forests, and in a torrent of wild animals.

On April 4, 1938, with both their divorces granted, Friederike and Peter Bally were married. They moved into the Ainsworth Hotel, several blocks from the museum. "Your name is next to mine on our marriage certificate," Peter told her, "but I've never thought of you as a 'Friederike.' You've filled me with great joy. If you agree, that's what I'd like to call you from now on—not Friederike, but Joy."

She nodded slightly, surprised, but then it seemed entirely right that she change not only her last name but her first, that she put the past behind her. "Yes," she answered Peter, "you can call me Joy."

They honeymooned by joining a three-month safari on the twenty-eight-mile-long Chyulu Hills in southeast Kenya. Formed by volcanic eruptions, the hills are unique in their vegetation pattern. Conditions vary from lava deposits, barren of any plant growth, to dense and luxuriant rainforest.

The expedition included a zoologist to study animal

life on Chyulu, a geologist to study the physical region, an entomologist to study insects, a paleontologist to study fossils, and Peter, as botanist, to study plants. Along with these five men were Friederike, introduced as Joy (the only woman), a kitchen crew, workers and porters from the Wakamba tribe, a field laboratory, a truck full of tents, and collapsible storage huts.

What had been forgotten on the expedition were bottles of drinking water. Under sweltering heat, the only freshwater spring on Chyulu had dried up to a slow trickle, filling just one four-gallon can each day. Pushing onward the expedition soon used up the spring water. Everyone suffered from dehydration until, on a patch of parched ground, a Wakamba porter discovered some old elephant footprints, or spoor, that held muddy, bug-infested water from the last rains. Repulsive as the black liquid looked, it was collected and boiled—and swallowed by all. Luckily, no one became ill, and as the expedition moved upward on the seven-thousand-foot-high hills, the air was suddenly filled with rain that, for days on end, soaked hair, clothing, and gear. "Famine to feast!" the cook kept repeating, catching the water on his tongue and racing, in celebration, around the small kerosene stove that was used to dry out plant specimens.

One morning as Peter was examining and labeling flowers, eight of the expedition members hiked nearby over rough ground, looking for scientific treasures. In the midst of their activities, a deafening crash sounded about fifty yards away, and a huge buffalo came rushing at them from a grove of sagebrush and trees. The buffalo's horns, streaked with dirt, framed its angry, red-lidded eyes.

Shouting and screaming, the safari members flung themselves outward like spokes of a wheel. Peter could be heard yelling at the top of his lungs. "Joy!" he screamed. "Run! Run for safety!"

And indeed, she did run—faster than in any childhood game. Only once did she look over her shoulder at the coarse brown hair of the buffalo, at the size of the body that came toward her like a speeding tank, at the sharp points of the horns. Gasping, she finally threw herself to the side, hitting the ground and rolling downward in somersaults into a stone-pocked gulley.

She lay on her stomach, her arms pinned beneath her. She heard the hooves of the buffalo drumming past her, then the furious snorts and grunts; she could feel the animal heat. She was sweating and bruised, and she was frightened, but as she turned onto her back—stones tearing her clothes—she felt a sense of exhilaration. *This,* she knew with absolute certainty, *was her place.* This continent, this Africa, this world of animals and nature, of battles between life and death. She wanted to immerse herself in it, to learn it well. It might continue to threaten her, it might even kill her, but it would be a home that would bring her meaning. It would bring her—yes!—joy.

CHAPTER 4

ALONG WITH SPECIMENS collected at Chyulu for the Coryndon Museum, Joy and Peter brought back two mementos. The first was a leaf from the amazing wild banana, or *musa,* tree, which turns the bitter sap in its trunk into pure drinking water as its fruit decays. The expedition members, thirsty again on the southwest hills, had collected forty-eight gallons of liquid from one *musa.*

The other memento was a wrinkled paper that had been torn into pieces and taped back together. Using some of Peter's coloring pencils, Joy had earlier sketched several plant specimens. Frustrated over the results, she ripped up the paper, but not before Peter, who drew extremely accurate illustrations, saw her work. "These sketches are good, Joy," he said, picking up the torn pieces. "You could do botanical drawing. I'm saving them."

In Nairobi Peter introduced Joy to some of his influential friends: Dr. V. van Someren, curator of the museum; Louis and Mary Leakey, world-famous anthropologists; and Dr. Arthur and Lady Muriel Jex-Blake, writers of *Gardening in East Africa*. Muriel Jex-Blake had an ornamental garden, a coffee farm, and horses she let Joy ride. Near Oma's age, Muriel took Joy under her wing. She was so impressed with Joy's sketches that she invited her to illustrate, in ink and paint, the latest edition of *Gardening in East Africa*.

"But I'm an amateur!" Joy said. "The plants you want to include grow from sea level to the mountains. I'd need to travel across Kenya. What if I didn't finish the assignment in time?"

"You'll finish," Muriel replied. "You have grit, energy, and skill. The art instruction in Vienna has polished you. You'll finish."

Joy began driving with Peter through a variety of Kenya's altitudes with easels, paint tubes, brushes, pens, and notebooks. She did her illustrations; he collected specimens. Sometimes Joy painted through the night by the pale flicker of a safari lamp, bitten by swarms of insects. When possible she covered herself with mosquito netting. She painted the blue-green delphinium, the ruby red everlasting, the scarlet gladiolus, and the giant, tree-sized groundsel with its golden flowers poised like praying hands. In the mountains snow protected plants from icy night winds until the midday sun warmed the flowers, thawing the snow on petals and stems.

Not only did Joy provide the Jex-Blakes with the art they needed, she completed her assignment ahead of schedule. She would illustrate all future editions of the gardening book. Muriel Jex-Blake arranged an exhibit of her work in Nairobi, bringing, to Joy's astonishment, a commission from the governor's wife to paint twenty flower pictures for General Jan Christiaan Smuts, the prime minister of South Africa. Eventually Joy was persuaded to submit her paintings to the Royal Horticultural Society in London, where she won the prestigious Grenfell Gold Medal.

One of the safaris undertaken with Peter and a guide, a cook, and Wakamba porters brought Joy on a climb of Mount Kenya, where she camped at twelve thousand feet above sea level to paint alpine flora—avoiding huge antelopes called elands who thundered out of the forest to feed on the grassland. In an arid section of Kenya, she and Peter went on a three-week safari to collect valuable medicinal plants, which laboratories would pulverize and sell to the public. And atop Mount Kilimanjaro, the highest point in Africa, Joy found a "most spectacular plant," a five-foot-high lobelia with rare mites crawling inside its flowers. Learning how to pack gear, climb steep faces of rock, and "decode" animal spoor, Joy felt less like a foreigner in Africa. On Mount Kilimanjaro, she and Peter climbed without ropes or ice picks, their pockets stuffed with raisins and chocolate. The greatest hardship was the very thin air above eighteen thousand feet. "We were obliged," Joy would write, "to rest after every four steps."

Lava lay in loose chunks by the foot of Kilimanjaro, but as Joy and Peter ascended, it became fine sand and then dust. Slowly, arduously, they finally reached the

19,340-foot-high crater on the third day of their climb. Staring down at the vast drop below them, they made their way to Kaiser Wilhelm Spitze Point, where they left their written names in a bottle to prove they'd reached the summit.

"I used to climb a bit in Europe," Joy told Peter. "I decided never to quit when conditions got hard."

"Not much quits in Africa," Peter said. "Not the heat or cold, not the monsoons, floods, fires, or dust storms, not the killings or birthings."

"Not the challenges," Joy replied.

A challenge soon arose for Joy that would not have surprised the Italian fortune-teller. While hiking with Peter, searching for wild orchids, she felt pain in her abdomen. Gamely, she kept walking, but when the pain increased, she went to lie down in the car. By the time Peter drove her back to the cottage they'd rented from Louis and Mary Leakey, she knew that she was having another miscarriage (though she hadn't even realized she was pregnant). Old feelings of loss consumed her; would she ever be cutting the stitches to let out the dresses she'd kept for a pregnancy?

To soothe the anguish of the miscarriage, Peter gave Joy a small male cairn terrier she named Pippin. The dog became her constant companion. Hiking with her, Pippin slept under mosquito netting on safaris, and in Nairobi he scampered across the Coryndon Museum, which had just hired Joy to paint pictures of the rare plants that scientists brought her. Pippin developed an unusual routine with his mistress: If Joy sang he joined in, howling at high or low pitch to match her tone. Standing up on her lap during renditions of "The Song of the Volga Boatmen" or arias from *Aïda,* Pippin followed the melodies so well that, according to Joy, "our duets became famous" among the local populace.

In September 1939, while Joy was helping the Leakeys reconstruct fragments of excavated bones, World War II broke out. The Axis powers, ignited by Germany's anti-Jewish dictator, Adolf Hitler, were pitted against the Allied powers, which later included the United States. Upset, Joy sometimes wished she were back in Vienna. Many of her friends there were either Jewish or as anti-Nazi as she; they might be in danger. "Hans Hofmann, my stepfather, must be pleased over the plight of the Jews," she said to the Leakeys.

Kenya, a British colony since 1895, was actually being threatened by the Italian brigades that occupied Ethiopia. Hundreds of Kenyan farmers formed their own army. One weekday, with gunfire exploding in the distance, Joy sat in the new house she and Peter had built, painting a rare white delphinium given to her by Muriel Jex-Blake. Suddenly the front door was pushed open and a uniformed policewoman strode into the parlor. "You are Joy Friederike Gessner von Klarwill Bally?"

Joy nodded.

"You will pack a small bag," the policewoman commanded. "You will be held in custody for the rest of the war." Joy was stunned. Surely the Kenyan government didn't think she was a Nazi. "May I just finish my painting?" she asked, as if the delphinium's white petals and velvety blue stamen could erase what was happening.

"Bring the silly flower with you," the policewoman said. "And hurry up! You and other prisoners will be kept in a convent until a permanent camp is ready."

Joy packed paints, brushes, a small canvas, and several items of clothing. Stiffly, she picked up Pippin as well as the delphinium. "I go *nowhere* without my dog," she said, glowering at the other woman.

"Then your dog is also under arrest," the policewoman said. "Maybe you'll both be deported."

Joy struggled down the front walkway—suitcase, flower, and Pippin clutched tightly. Looking behind her, she tried to memorize the view of the house amid its dark grove of fig trees. Her face, tanned by the African sun, showed strain and confusion but no fear. Even though she didn't understand what accusations were being made against her, and she might not be able to live in Kenya any longer, she was still determined and "unruly" enough not to cry.

THE GROUP OF prisoners on the train with Joy were all under wartime suspicion. From a way station they were trucked to the detaining camp hidden eight thousand feet above the Rift Valley. Everyone slept on the lava-strewn ground; the toilet, in a ramshackle outhouse, was a gaping hole in the dirt. With one of her painting tools, Joy carved an eating bowl for Pippin from a chunk of soft firewood, and she shared her food rations with him. He buoyed the spirits of the other prisoners when they were forced by a guard to exercise. Just as he'd performed his duets with Joy, Pippin jumped when the prisoners were commanded to jump, hopped when they hopped, and ran with them in a circle. "For first time since we here," one woman said to Joy in broken English, "I laugh, from your dog."

Peter was outraged at Joy's arrest. He sought help immediately from his friends, but two weeks passed before the governor allowed Joy's release. The cause of her arrest proved to be the Jex-Blakes, who had naively told police that some of Joy's houseguests spoke German. Called before government officials in Nairobi, Joy pledged her loyalty to the Allies. And she knew the Jex-Blakes had meant her no harm. To show her affection, she gave Muriel the finished painting of the white delphinium, refusing to accept payment.

Joy was even more generous to Ziebel, her ex-husband, who had fled with his mother from the anti-Jewish fever in Europe and arrived exhausted and penniless in Kenya. Quietly Joy sent Ziebel money she earned from her flower paintings. In time he was selling cars once again and was deeply grateful to Joy for her kindness.

In July 1940, nearly two years after the outbreak of World War II, Peter fell ill with kidney disease. His doctor advised prolonged rest. Since the war had temporarily halted flights to Europe, Peter decided to spend several months alone in South Africa. One of Joy's friends, Alys Reece, heard of Peter's recuperation plans and thought it would be a good time to invite Joy to help care for her three children. Alys's husband supervised Kenya's Northern Frontier District (NFD), a semidesert area of 120,000 square miles. In the Reeces' cabin on Mount Marsabit, Joy was enthralled by the view of hills, plains, and valleys. To the north lived members of the Boran tribe, who rode wild mountain horses; in the forests gray lichen plants hung like streamers of confetti from the trees. Joy promised herself she would fully explore this wilderness one day.

Each morning she took the Reece children to see the antelope—large greater kudus and smaller klipspringers and bushbucks—that gathered at a nearby bubbling spring. After breakfast, as the freezing mountain winds died down, Alys tutored the children inside the cabin while Joy, a hot-water bottle on her lap, painted the flowers of Marsabit. Soon the sun scorched the flatlands, and Joy and the children would hike down to the Kaisut Desert, marveling over its rare species of mole rats, whose skins were so transparent that their veins, arteries, and organs were visible.

Joy missed seeing Peter, yet part of her was detached from him, as if she found herself safer among the flowers, antelope, and mole rats than in her human relationships. Often she lay under the trees, listening to opera music from the Reeces' record player. She kept a diary, describing her enduring love for music. In Vienna, she wrote, she'd often walked home after a performance of Richard Strauss's opera *Der Rosenkavalier* "too full of the music to bear anyone's company."

When Peter returned to Nairobi, reuniting with Joy, he seemed physically well but weary. He and Joy traveled to the small outpost of Garissa, about two hundred miles northeast of Nairobi, where he tested rocks for pigments that might be used to camouflage war tents and cars. Garissa, near Kenya's largest river, the Tana, had its own police inspector and officers, the only Europeans in the area. Willy Hale, district commissioner of Garissa, invited Joy and Peter to join his family for Christmas. Other Europeans would be guests of the Hales, too, among them a "highly unusual chap" from the Game Department named George Adamson.

On Christmas Eve, Joy helped Morna Hale, Willy's wife, stuff pheasants and listened to stories about the other guests, especially George Adamson, who had not yet arrived. "He's a hero in Kenya," Morna said. "Not long ago he was attacked in the bush by a lion. He barely escaped and, though almost dead, he still cleaned his own wounds. That night he became delirious from blood loss and malaria, but somehow he saw an elephant charging his tent. A much better shot than his men, he yelled for them to prop him up on his cot and, shaking with fever, he actually shot the elephant through the head."

"My great-grandfather would have approved," Joy said. "He believed if something had to be done, you did it—no matter what."

That evening Joy sat with Peter and the other guests on the wind-cooled roof of the Hales' house. She wore a silver evening gown from Vienna, though it looked strange in the desert setting. With no snow, carolers, or stores filled with gifts to mark Christmas, she wanted to at least look festive. A sprig of berries decorated her hair; an amulet from Peter hung at her neck. Sipping wine, she watched a group of Somali and Riverine tribesmen prepare for a *ngoma,* or dance, on the ground below. Then the men began to scatter and sway, a drumlike sound rising from them in almost perfect unison.

"What's happening?" Joy asked Morna.

"Oh, look!" Morna answered. "The dance is for George—and, at last, he's here!"

Gazing at the procession of camels slowly approaching the house, Joy saw a man riding a two-humped camel at the head of the line. Thin, with sandy-colored hair, he had a beard and mustache, and he grinned at her as if he knew her. His chest, face, and arms were browner than his safari shorts; a pipe was stuck behind his left ear. Astride his camel, George Adamson somehow didn't seem to Joy like the people she lived among now or in the past. He seemed, she decided as she smiled back at him—Peter at her side—like one of the great beasts of Africa. He seemed like a tawny-haired lion himself.

CHAPTER 5

WITHIN A MONTH Joy and Peter joined a camel safari
led by George Adamson. They stayed with George until
they reached the town of Bura, then went to the port of
Lamu, where Peter searched for plants. On the safari Joy
noticed George's silence; his main replies were "Oh,"
"Really," or "How extraordinary." He did, however,
talk to Joy about wild animals living in the Northern
Frontier District (NFD). She learned of the reticulated
giraffe, its dark spots patterned closely together; the
oryx, an antelope with long pointed horns; and the
blue-legged ostrich, whose kicks delivered deadly
blows. George said that he lived in the hills outside Isiolo, an NFD village with a few *duka*s, or shops, a
church, and a prison.

When Joy first mounted and rode a camel on the
safari, she felt regal perched between its two scratchy
humps. Under her was a makeshift saddle of grass matting; above her was a sun so hot she grew increasingly

sleepy. By the lunch break, sliding down to the ground, she found she could barely move. Never wanting to seem weak or whiny, she'd ignored a continuing discomfort on the ride, but it appeared that the saddle's damp matting had rubbed her back raw and bloody. Peter and George put disinfectant on her wounds. Though she was in great pain if she bent down, she refused to complain and would not agree to stop the safari.

The next day she sketched desert trails and craggy rocks in the NFD. George taught her how to attract crocodiles by calling, "Imm, imm, imm." Curled under mosquito netting at night, she heard the roaring of lions and the strange cackling of hyenas. When the camel procession reached Lamu, where she and Peter were greeted by white-robed Arabs living among African tribes, she regretted having to leave the safari.

Peter gathered plants in Lamu as Joy sat at the harbor, drawing the small boats that brought spices, dates, and Persian carpets from Arabia to exchange for local goods. In February Joy returned with Peter to Nairobi. The camel safari was still on her mind when, by accident, she met George Adamson on the street. His eyes gazed deeply into hers, but he said little. Only after being prodded to sit on a bench with her did he mumble a few sentences. He had not planned, he said, to ever see her again. The truth was, he continued, he'd fallen in love with her, but wouldn't try to break up her marriage.

In the next days, Joy could hardly concentrate on the smallest task. She was attached to Peter and knew that his European upbringing meshed with hers. But she was also drawn to George, who didn't even share her love of music and art. Peter was like her silver Christmas dress, elegant and refined. George, born in India, was of the earth and nature, more primitive and plain. She decided to ask Peter for a divorce, but she thought she might be crazy. She went to Muriel Jex-Blake, pouring out her uncertainty.

"Joy," said her friend, "you have intense emotions. Sometimes they stifle your common sense. But I hope for your happiness. If you choose to go with George, I won't abandon you."

Peter had tried to understand Joy's feelings, but she was too changeable for him. First she wanted a divorce; then she didn't. She would stay with him; she must go. Unable to depend on the marriage, Peter retreated, leaving Kenya for Ethiopia. Joy hired a lawyer, telling George she'd soon be free, but she kept writing letters to Peter. Finally, too upset to stay in Nairobi during the divorce proceedings, she took a cook, a gun bearer, and Pippin to the marshlands of Mount Kenya to camp and paint flowers. A nearby farmer agreed that his two workers could occasionally bring her supplies on horseback. "Put your tents under the row of trees dividing forest from marshland," said the farmer. "You can climb to safety if elephants or buffalo bother you."

One buffalo came each night to rub against the thick tent canvas, terrifying Pippin, but it always moved onward. Other problems developed from the nine-foot lobelia plant that Joy and the gun bearer brought into camp for her to paint. Everyone's eyelids, nostrils, and lips swelled and their stomachs churned with nausea. Joy finally remembered that Peter had vomited for hours from a poisonous substance from inside a lobelia identified as caustic latex.

George visited Joy's camp on weekends. Though he felt guilty about Peter, he was nevertheless deeply in love. He asked Joy to marry him, yet even after the divorce from Peter was granted, Joy was torn between the two men. George tried to be patient with her, but the waiting seemed unbearable "Either you choose a life with me—or you should go back to Peter," he said.

Finally, on Monday, January 17, 1944, three days before her thirty-fourth birthday, Joy married George Adamson in the district commissioner's office in Nairobi. At George's house in Isiolo, her piano was put in the main room; some of the seventy flower paintings from her four months on Mount Kenya were hung beside a buffalo skull that George had preserved. Along with Joy, George, and Pippin, the house was constantly shared with one or more orphaned animals that Joy brought in: baby giraffes, lions, and elephants, even tiny, newborn weaverbirds. Joy rescued and sheltered, at various times, twenty mongooses. Small and ferretlike, they were affectionate and house-trained enough to sleep on her bed, but fierce enough to kill poisonous snakes. Joy's favorite mongoose, whom she named Metternich after an Austrian statesman, had nosebleeds if he was upset.

The work George performed as assistant game warden of the NFD involved enforcing government laws about animals. If he had to kill an animal to protect human beings, George didn't hesitate, but he hated killing for sport. He arrested and jailed poachers, both native and tourist, who trespassed illegally into established wildlife reserves, hunted game without obtaining licenses, or killed for profit any animals who lived in government-established "no kill" areas. Poachers slaughtered elephants for their ivory tusks; shot rhinoceroses, or rhinos, for their horns; and killed giraffes for their hides. George had arrested hundreds of poachers and, according to one government official, was "nearly killed [each year] by some wild animal or other." He made friends, however, with many animals, walking among them as if he belonged.

The first experience that Joy had with George's work arose when the remains, mostly socks and parts of feet, of a group of escaped prisoners were found near Nairobi. A pride of eight lions lived in the area, and the Game Department asked George to kill the entire pride. Joy accompanied her new husband as he placed raw meat on the ground for bait. Vultures began to circle in the sky, bringing in the lions. From a car hidden in the undergrowth, Joy watched all eight lions tearing at the bait. She was nearer than she had ever been to any lion, awed by the golden bodies and thick, beautiful manes. Suddenly, in the bursts of George's gunfire, the lions leaped away with groans and whimpers. One by one, they collapsed, their mouths open. Though she had known what was going to happen, Joy raced out of the car toward the heaving bodies. She could hardly pull any air into her lungs. She was remembering the buck she had shot when she was fifteen.

"Why? Why was it necessary to kill them?" she shouted at George. "The prisoners took their chances of being devoured!"

"Most lions," George replied, "don't ever attack humans unless starved or injured. But these had become man-eaters. They'd have killed again."

Turning calmly away, George asked his crew to transport the dead lions by truck to the Game Department headquarters, to be officially counted. Joy wondered, her head throbbing, if all the days ahead would be marked by death. As she thought of Peter, who had been so gentle with his botanical specimens, she realized that the plants and flowers were also, in their own way, slain. She waited in the car for George to finish his work, looking up at the green velvet of the trees edged with pale light. A silence more profound than George's silence lay over the faded echoes of the dying lions. Never before, Joy would write, had she been quite so conscious of how precious life could be, "not just our own lives, but the lives around us."

ON SAFARIS, Joy and George were an unbeatable team, willing to undergo hardship and eager for adventure. George saw that Joy could keep up with him and was an ideal safari mate as they immersed themselves in the rigors of Africa's changing seasons and the cycles of her wildlife; the nesting, mating, birthing, and caring for offspring;

the hunting, migrating, and claiming of territory; and, finally, the dying. George could read spoor—the footprints or other trails left by animals—like a master decoder. He never wore a watch; he used the sun for his clock and the moon for his calendar. His life had not yet been invaded by news broadcasts or the noise of commercial airplanes. If Joy seemed moody or difficult to him, he was as tolerant of her as he was of the high-spirited animals he tamed. Joy exceeded her own expectations of toughness. Once, she rode on a camel safari with a fever of 104 degrees, wrapping herself in wet sheets against the blistering sun. Another time she sketched a leopard near her tent without calling for aid.

Drama, Joy saw, was a part of Africa's landscape. At times swarms of locusts stripped Isiolo of vegetation, flew at her eyes, and buzzed in her ears. During an especially cold April, when George was off arresting poachers at the Ethiopian border, she joined an expedition that stumbled into a mountain blizzard. All night she clung, wet and freezing, to a narrow ledge above a raging river.

She was only really frightened by adult elephants. She held George's torch one sundown when he shot a charging elephant, and found she was too frightened to swallow. Elephants are the African animal most aware of death. Some bury the bones of dead herd members. Others, if they kill a human being, return every day in mourning to the place of death.

When hiking or climbing with George, Joy painted and drew flowers, as she had with Peter. By 1945 she'd created nearly five hundred flower paintings and several hundred line drawings. More than fifty of her paintings and drawings were reproduced in *Gardening in East Africa* and *Some Wild Flowers of Kenya,* thirty-one appeared in *Kenya Trees and Shrubs* and *The Indigenous Trees of Uganda Protectorate,* and many were purchased by the newly re-named Nairobi (Coryndon) Museum and by the Fort Jesus Museum in Mombasa. Because most of these flow-ers had never before been accurately rendered, Joy's work stands today as a major achievement in botany as well as art.

Soon she began collecting rare species of insects, fish, and reptiles to send to museums, and traveled across parts of the continent to paint portraits of men, women, and children from many of the fifty or more main tribes of Africa. To the Nairobi Museum, she sent a black fish with iridescent blue spots that had never before been seen in East Africa, and a chameleon with white feet. Scientists at first marked these finds "unknown species."

Joy's first portrait was of the *liwali,* the sheik, or head, of the Arabs in the town of Malindi. Dressed in a deep blue indigo robe embroidered with gold, and carrying a silver sword, the *liwali* wore an elaborate turban. With Pippin on her lap, Joy labored over the sketch for seven hours. She was pleased that the *liwali* rewarded her with a smile.

At the Ethiopian and Uganda-Kenya borders, Joy painted naked Kadam warriors who had molded their hair into huge hoods ornamented with ostrich feathers. Though the warriors couldn't speak Joy's language, they agreed to sit for her when she pointed to her easel and gave them tobacco and sugar. She painted a Turkana warrior, known for drinking animal blood, who had punctured his nose and lips with metal plugs, and a chief of the Elgeyo tribe, face streaked with white paste, who wore a robe of blue monkey fur.

Joy described to George by letter how many of Africa's tribes, influenced by Christian missionaries, were forsaking their costumes and rituals. Their hand embroidery, she wrote, will be replaced by sewing machines. Their walking sticks will become bicycles. If she painted these tribespeople as they were then, Joy said, a visible record would exist of their culture.

Joy's first official commission for a tribal painting came from a deputy at the town of Kapsabet. Would she do a life-size oil portrait, she was asked, of a Nandi tribesman to hang in the Memorial Hall? Although she'd rarely used oils, she agreed. The portrait—for which she was paid the equivalent of thirty dollars—caught the attention of a district commissioner who promised to persuade Kenya's Governor and Legislative Council to pay Joy to keep painting tribespeople. In January 1949, to her great delight, the government offered her a contract for £1,000, or approximately $2,000. In twelve to eighteen months, she was to deliver 132 portraits from twenty-two African tribes. To handle such an assignment, she would have to buy a truck and hire a driver, but she could take Pippin with her. Though she'd be spending time away from George, they both agreed that the work was important.

On the day Joy signed the government contract and

had it delivered to Nairobi, a sandstorm burst out of the desert near Wajir, 150 miles from Isiolo. Sand filled Joy's mouth, matted her hair, and clogged the wings of birds so they fell in thousands from the sky. Breathing through her nose, spitting some of the sand onto the ground, Joy stood in her khaki shorts and shirt beneath a daum-palm tree. "Pippin!" she called out, watching the little dog plow forward through the sand gusts until she could pick him up and cradle him against her chest. "I'm a working painter now, Pippin!" she said, not letting the storm ruin her excitement. "For the first time in my life, I'll be able to pay my own bills. And I can use some of the money for animals."

Wiping the sand from Pippin's face and cleaning his ears, Joy suddenly thought of Oma's brooch of the goddess Diana, which was nestled in a cloth in the house at Isiolo. Joy wished she could talk on this day to her grandmother. "Oma," she would say, "your brooch *did* bring me strength. Maybe your faith in me has come true. Maybe your Friederike, your restless granddaughter who is now Joy Adamson, has something good that she can do."

CHAPTER 6

BY THE LATE 1940s, Joy had lost both Oma and Pippin. A message from Europe, where World War II had been won by the Allies in 1945, informed her that Oma was dead and that her stepfather, Hans Hofmann, was imprisoned as a Nazi sympathizer. With Vienna occupied by Allied forces and not easily entered, Joy booked passage on a ship to England. Nine years had passed since she'd seen her mother or sisters. The night before embarking, she was, as George wrote in his own diary, "terribly upset," first over Oma's death, then over leaving him in Africa, but he encouraged her to stay abroad as long as she wanted.

Among bombed-out buildings in Hampstead, England, Joy rented a room and applied at a government office for a permit to visit Vienna. Postwar suspicion was everywhere, however, and the permit was denied. After applying again, she visited friends in England, sharing with them remembrances of Oma. She also consulted a new psychoanalyst. Peter Bally, in London on business, escorted her to the opera, careful not to overstep his bounds. Never one to waste time, Joy signed up for a portrait painting class at London's Slade school. To her surprise, some tribal sketches that she had casually shown to the London editor of *Geographical Magazine* were accepted for publication.

Joy received a month's permit to Vienna. After crossing the English Channel, she took the train to Vienna and was met at the station by her sister Traute, who had divorced and was now a journalist. They drove to visit their mother and Dorle, both of whom seemed depressed. "Mama," Joy said, "the dress you're wearing hung in your closet years ago. Do you need money?"

"No," her mother replied, "money is not my trouble. I grieve over the thousands of Vienna's houses that are destroyed. Garbage fills the streets here, and Russian soldiers loiter on doorsteps. My hope is in waiting for Hans's release from jail."

The Russians had erected statues of Joseph Stalin and Lenin in Vienna's main squares, alongside debris from the bombings. When Joy and her mother went to sketch trees in the park, Russian soldiers harrassed them. Joy tried shooing them away with both German and broken English, but she and her mother soon put away their notebooks and pens and went home.

The majority of Joy's Jewish friends had been killed during the war; only a few, such as Ziebel, escaped the Nazis. Joy learned, in shock, that Seifenmühle, her childhood home, was gone, covered by the largest reservoir in Czechoslovakia. She wrote to George of the nightmare that had descended on Europe. Millions had died, many in concentration camps. Museums and libraries had been bombed or looted—paintings slashed, artifacts stolen, books burned in outdoor bonfires.

After placing bouquets of roses on Oma's grave in Vienna, Joy finally bid her family good-bye. George met her when she arrived back in Kenya and drove her to his brother Terence's farm in Limuru, where George had left Pippin. Horrified, she found her dog chained to a table leg. He dragged himself, whimpering, across the floor to lick her hands. Weeks passed before he seemed lively, but never again would he sing duets with his mistress.

In the spring, Pippin suffered from nosebleeds. Joy drove him to a vet for medication, but he barely rallied. She brought him to the foot of Mount Kenya, where she painted the Mbere tribe, and watched him closely. One afternoon as the Mbere men and women began one of their frenzied dances, Pippin lay at Joy's feet, panting. By sundown he was too weak to walk with her in the grass.

Luckily George arrived for the weekend, taking turns with Joy at holding and stroking Pippin. On the second night, Pippin died, a tiny veteran of safari life. In his years with Joy, he had braved ice and wind on the mountains, chilling storms in the forests, and smothering heat on the plains. After she buried him under a forest tree, Joy wrote, "With him, I buried part of myself."

She went on several safaris to distract herself. In the

Wajir desert, she painted Somali tribespeople beside their limestone water wells. With George, she visited the magnificent Chanler Falls on the Uaso Nyiro River, and helped him search for poachers at Lorian Swamp. They encountered there a drought so severe that the ground was littered with the rotting bodies of dead cattle, camels, sheep, and goats. Somali tribespeople had stumbled for weeks among the dead animals, desperately seeking water. Camels and elephants were stuck in dried mud, slowly starving. At last rain fell on Lorian Swamp, but Joy, still missing Pippin, grew ill from malaria and tick-borne fever. She consulted a doctor in Nairobi, who treated her with arsenic injections; she recovered but she suffered a third miscarriage, again unaware that she'd been in early pregnancy.

Perhaps it was destiny, then, that brought Joy and George in February 1956 to track poachers in the Kinna area of the NFD. While Joy stayed in the makeshift camp with her newest orphaned animal—Pati, a rock hyrax the size of a large guinea pig—George and a crew of men went to shoot a lion that had eaten a Boran tribesman. Hours later, driving back into camp, George had a lion skin tied to the hood of his car.

"You found the killer lion," Joy said.

"Not sure," George replied. "The skin is from a lioness who charged us. We had to shoot her. I feel bad about it."

"Come in the tent. You probably need rest."

"No," George said, not moving. "I've got something in the car for you. Go look."

Joy strode toward the car, opened the rear door, and gasped. *"Cubs!"* she said. "They look almost newborn! The lioness you killed was their mother? I bet she charged you because she was protecting her children."

"That's what we decided," George said quietly. "Would you want to take care of the three cubs? They're probably female."

Joy stared at the golden bundles of fur, touching the tiny pink noses, noticing the birth film still covering the eyes. If she adopted the cubs, they would consider *her* their mother when they could see, a process of emotional attachment called imprinting that had been demonstrated in the early 1950s by zoologist Konrad Lorenz. Bonded to a human, Joy realized, the cubs would never learn to hunt well enough to survive in the wild. But at least she could save their lives, as she'd saved the other orphaned animals she'd sheltered. Later she might send them to zoos. Having lost a baby with each of her three marriages, she felt a sudden, immense affection for these fuzzy waifs nuzzling each other in the car.

"Let's bring them inside," she said, smiling.

Sweeping two of the cubs into her arms, leaving the third one for George, Joy hurried toward the tent. She would never forget that February day in the NFD, nor, in the years to come, would countless people throughout the world. "Little did I know," Joy would write of the lion cubs she and George had named Lustica, Big One, and Elsa, "that on that morning my whole life would be changed forever."

———

JOY, GEORGE, and Nuru, a Somali worker, took care of the "triplets," though the real "nanny" became Pati, the orphaned rock hyrax. When Lustica, Big One, and Elsa were brought home to Isiolo, Pati began guarding and disciplining them. If they got into mischief, she stared them down until they behaved, and was brave enough to do so even when they outgrew her in size. At night Pati wrapped herself around Joy's neck like a fur and, when content, ground her teeth together with little clicking noises. She had developed such a liking for alcohol that she learned to push over a bottle of bourbon, pull out the cork, and lap up some contents.

A pen was built for the cubs, though they were also allowed in the house. Before she could buy nursing bottles or collect advice about feeding them, Joy used rubber tubing from her wireless telegraph machine to hold unsweetened canned milk, cod liver oil, and glucose. The cubs were given raw, minced meat when they were approximately three months old. Joy made sure that Elsa, the tiniest cub, had enough to eat before her sisters pushed her away; in the bush, Elsa might have been the runt that didn't survive. Had the cubs' mother lived, she would have fed her babies for a year with food she had swallowed and regurgitated, and would have taught them to hunt alone by the age of two.

For the first time since she'd come to live in Africa, Joy didn't feel compelled to go on safaris. The cubs were deeply satisfying to her. In the evenings, with Pati curled around her neck, she would take Elsa onto her lap. Elsa would suck happily on Joy's thumbs and burrow against her chest. Even when the cubs began to playfully stalk their human guardians, flying through the air to land on someone's back, Joy didn't mind if she was the "prey." Knocked down, she would merely shake her head. And if potato sacks or tires didn't entertain the cubs, and Big One stole laundry off the clothesline, or Elsa toppled the plates and glasses that the cook had put out for dinner, Joy would just laugh. To keep any sort of order, she finally had to shut all three cubs out of the house. Lustica, however, sneaked inside by turning doorknobs, opening handles, and moving aside bolts with her teeth.

Across much of Kenya at this time, laughter became a rarity, stifled by rage from groups of Kikuyu tribesmen calling themselves Mau Mau. Inspired by Johnston "Jomo" Kenyatta, a European-educated Kikuyu who worked for his country's independence from Britain and equal rights for his tribe, the Mau Mau had chosen violence over Kenyatta's attempts at peaceful negotiation. In 1949, Kikuyu turned against Kikuyu, some embracing the Mau Mau rebellion, others resisting it. Mau Mau gangs slaughtered both Europeans and Africans, using axes, knives, and a lethal poison, *orogi,* on arrows. Among the Caucasians in Africa, the Mau Mau revolt was called the Emergency.

Never had Kenya witnessed such brutality. Policemen roamed the streets of towns and cities, roadblocks and ambushes were set up to capture Mau Mau gangs, and barbed wire and sirens were installed at many homes. By the time Joy and George brought their three lion cubs home to Isiolo, George had already organized twelve

Joy and the three baby lions:
Elsa, Lustica, and Big One

Elsa at six months

Joy and Elsa cheek to cheek

Lustica, Elsa's sister, opening a door latch with her teeth

Elsa alone after her sisters have been sent to the zoo in Rotterdam

George training Elsa to hunt for guinea hens

Using a blanket, Elsa learns to drag her "kill,"
a skill other lions learn from their mothers.

Elsa dragging a dead antelope

Truck troubles on safari: Supplies usually were rescued.

George and Elsa resting in camp

Joy and Elsa in a "lion" hug

Time-out in the bush for Joy and Elsa

Elsa in repose on top of
the Land Rover

Joy and one of the several baby elephants she rescued and sheltered

Elsa's antics among the dinner dishes

Elsa trying to carry the first fish catch back to camp

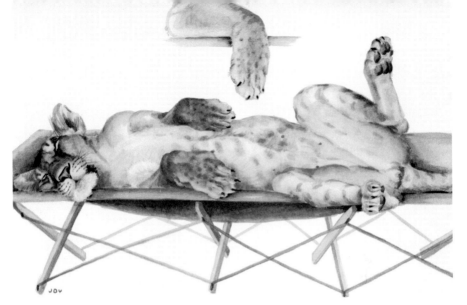

This painting of Elsa on a camp bed
is one of several that Joy made of Elsa.

Elsa traveling in comfort on safari

Gloriosa virescens, one of Joy's several hundred
botanical paintings. Joy was awarded the Grenfell
Gold Medal by the Royal Horticultural Society
in London for her botanical art.

An African warrior posing for
one of Joy's tribal paintings

Joy's painting of a Turkana warrior.
Nearly four hundred of Joy's tribal
paintings were purchased by the
Kenyan government, and many hang
in the National Museums of Kenya.

Elsa and her three cubs: Jespah, Gopa, and Little Elsa

Elsa nudging Jespah affectionately

Elsa's grave at Meru Park

The camp crew readying the cages to move Elsa's cubs from Meru Park

A dejected Jespah on his journey from Meru

Feeding time for Penny, the leopard

Pippa, the cheetah, playing
with a hanging bag

Joy with a handful of leopard cub

Joy watching two of the camp crew make friends with Pippa

Joy offering water to Whity, one of Pippa's cubs

Penny with her three-day-old cubs. Note her tracking collar.

Penny at rest,
but on the alert

policemen on Somali ponies as an "Adamson Force" to hunt Mau Mau. By 1956, when the rebellion was crushed, he had been promoted to senior game ranger of the NFD.

After defeat of the Mau Mau, world sympathies were no longer with the rebels. People were too frightened by the violence. Kenyatta had been jailed in a reaction against the Kikuyus. "Much of Kenya's innocence," Joy said, "is gone."

"Nothing stays the same," George replied.

Unexpected change had always followed Joy like a shadow. She had changed her youthful pursuits in Europe, and had changed husbands and homelands. In the constant round of animals living with her in Africa, however, her mothering of Elsa, Lustica, and Big One had, in many ways, altered her life most deeply, turning it upside down.

At five months old the cubs were roaming the woods, climbing trees, and dragging sheets with their mouths, as adult lions drag their kills. Together they slept in a heavy wire pen with a new addition of rock and sand, safe from attack by hyenas, jackals, elephants, and wild lions. Yet it slowly became obvious that they were growing too large to remain at Isiolo. Joy read of the humane conditions at the Rotterdam-Blydorp Zoo in Holland and wrote to the zoo's director, asking if he would accept the cubs. When he agreed, she balked at her own idea. "I can't let them all go," she told George. "I can't lose all my babies. We could send two of the cubs, but one must stay with us—at least for a while."

It was Elsa, runt of the litter, who had most won Joy's heart. And it was Elsa, still leaping onto Joy's lap and happily sucking her thumbs, who would remain at Isiolo. Arrangements were made to fly Lustica and Big One to the zoo. First Joy and George accustomed the two cubs to riding and eating in a truck. In several weeks the cubs were jumping delightedly into their traveling "playpen," waiting for it to roll down the road.

On the day of the flight to Holland, Joy tucked soft sandbags into the rear of the truck to make the cubs comfortable on their ride to the airport. Giving them chunks of raw meat after they leaped inside, she and George gently closed the wire-sided carriage area. For once Joy matched George in silence. Feeling that she was betraying two of her children, she climbed mutely into the truck to sit with the cubs, pulling them to her while George drove. She pressed the back of her hand against her mouth, stifling a moan at the sight of Elsa dashing down the driveway as if to say, "Wait for me! Don't leave me behind!" A bewildered and dejected Elsa soon sat on the dirt road with, according to Joy, "the most mournful expression in her eyes" as she watched the truck in which her "parents" and sisters were disappearing.

At the airport Lustica and Big One tried to hold on to Joy with their paws. They were placed in crates that were hoisted onto the plane. The director of the zoo had agreed to send a cable when the cubs arrived safely. Standing on the runway, wind hitting them like a fist, Joy and George could not have known that, in three years, Joy would actually visit the cubs at the zoo, finding them healthy, happy, and quite willing to be stroked. Nor could Joy have guessed that in several days, when George went on to Nairobi on business and she returned to Isiolo, she would find a determined Elsa waiting for her in the middle of the driveway instead of romping through the woods as usual.

That morning, according to Nuru, the Somali worker, Elsa had refused to move from the driveway, or to eat, or to be distracted. She was showing behavior that would eventually give the world amazing new information about the intelligence of lions. Head held high, eyes focused steadily down the road to look for what had been lost, Elsa—born in the wilds of Africa—had known on exactly which day, out of three days and two nights, her imprinted "mother," if not her entire family, was coming home.

CHAPTER 7

FOR WEEKS after Joy and George had returned separately to Isiolo, Elsa searched for her sisters in the bush around the house. She also followed after Joy and George as if afraid they would disappear again. Joy decided to take Elsa on safari, hoping a change of scenery would calm her. Before leaving, however, she wrote to Louis Leakey, the anthropologist who was a trustee for Kenya's national parks and who'd become a good friend. No facility existed in Africa, Joy reminded Leakey, to hold animals either orphaned or driven out of their territory when it was slated for farming or forestry. No haven was provided by any country for needy animals waiting to be sent to zoos or rerouted to new surroundings. Would Louis, Joy asked, use his influence to help her organize an animal refuge?

Government officials at Isiolo, contacted by Leakey, supported Joy's idea for a national orphanage and agreed to give her fifty acres of land outside town. But other authorities wanted the location nearer Nairobi. After much haggling, the Nairobi Animal Orphanage, the first of its kind in the world, was established on Langata Road, Nairobi. It was eventually supervised by Louis Leakey's son, Richard, director of Kenya's Wildlife Service.

With plans for the orphanage in progress, Joy and George packed up their gear and took Elsa on safari. Often moving through the bush alone, George checked for poachers by keeping track of the relative sizes of animal herds. He was charged by lions, elephants, and buffalo, and snapped at by crocodiles in the lakes where he bathed. Poachers shot at him with poisoned arrows, and only his skill at living in the bush saved him from being mauled or killed. Back at camp he recounted his escapes to Joy, and described them in his diary; sometimes he revealed them later to his brother Terence over a glass of whiskey.

From a safari along the Uaso Nyiro River, Joy and George took Elsa by truck to the eastern coast at the Somali border, then to Lake Rudoph in northern Kenya. Although lions prefer familiar territory, Elsa became a fine traveler, ranging out from camp seven to eight hours each day. She loved the water and played her own games, splashing Joy or dunking her under the waves. Pacing the shore, she showed delight at cuffing her parents on the ankles—landing them flat on their backs. Yet she gave Joy and George unending affection, licking them, rubbing her head against them, and making soft noises of appreciation. If she broke the "family rules," terrifying one of the donkeys by pouncing on it, or spreading mud over the breakfast table, she amazed everyone by soon acting like an ashamed child come to its senses, using every trick she knew to bring approval and laughter.

When Elsa was one year old, Joy and George took her to the coastal town of Kiunga. On the beach she jumped after a coconut George swung for her on a rope and chased hundreds of pink crabs that pinched her nose. Crawling with belly close to the ground, she stalked herds of giraffes or nipped at an elephant's heels, never having been taught by a lioness mother that elephants can trample lions to death. What her foster family could teach her, they did—and Pati filled in some gaps.

Pati, however, was suddenly felled by heatstroke. Though George gave her sips of brandy to strengthen her, her heartbeat was uneven. Lying in Joy's arms, she tried to grind her teeth—her old sign of contentment— but soon lapsed into a coma and died. "Over seven years we had her with us," Joy said to George as Pati was buried. "How she loved Lustica, Big One, and Elsa! After Pippin died, she was my only friend on painting trips. Now, among the pets I've had, I grieve for Hasi, Pippin, and Pati."

It was at Kiunga that George nearly became an addition to Joy's grief. One sundown, while Joy was out walking, he had such a severe reaction to medicine he'd swallowed for malaria that he believed he was sinking into insanity or death. He demanded that his crew hide his guns and knives so he wouldn't hurt himself or others. Then he cried out Joy's name.

Though their marriage was fused by a mutual devotion to safari life, Joy and George's relationship had never been easy. Joy resented George's solitary nature and stubborness, and he was stung by her mood swings, never sure if she was happy. Sometimes she still seemed to long for Peter Bally or would ardently play the piano George had bought her, ignoring his presence. Yet on the evening of his frightening delirium, it was only Joy that George wanted with him—confident that, somehow, she'd save him. When he heard her voice, he experienced an immense sense of tenderness and relief. "She came," he would write in his diary, having recovered by morning from the drug reaction, "and at once I felt... as if a great burden had been suddenly lifted from my head."

For Joy, having Elsa with her after Pati's death and George's crisis was strongly comforting. If the sun was savagely hot on safari, she greased Elsa's paws so they wouldn't get burned. If mountain winds and temperatures were icy, she brought Elsa into her tent at night, covering her with a blanket and lying awake to re-cover her if the blanket fell off. Elsa, in turn, seemed deeply grateful for the loving care, licking Joy's arm or face. Back at Isiolo, Joy hiked in the mornings with Elsa over flatlands and through forests and, in the afternoons, sat with her under a daum-palm tree, sketching or photographing her. Side by side, they might nap on a canvas bed. A stranger coming upon them would have gaped at the sight of the blond woman and the tawny lion wrapped about each other in such peaceful repose.

As the months passed, Elsa grew toward a lion's full

weight of approximately three hundred pounds; she would now need at least fifty acres in which to roam. She began going off by herself. She usually returned by nightfall, but if she was gone longer, Joy went looking for her, worried she might have been attacked by wild lions or other animals. Joy spent hours in the bush calling Elsa by name or tracking her spoor. Searching the nearby hills, she would climb over dangerously loose rocks or crusty lava deposits that might have slipped or cracked, and could have hurled Joy to her death. But after nineteen years in Africa, Joy was nearly as skilled a bushman as George. Game warden Gerry Dalton, one of George's friends, said Joy could "outswim, outwalk, and outclimb any man" and was "utterly fearless."

Inside herself, however, Joy remained the little girl of Seifenmühle who had refused to cry when her mother served Hasi for soup or her father so cruelly squeezed her hand. To her, animals continued to seem a safer place for her affections than humans. By 1958, when Elsa was two years old, Joy's attachment to her lion child was profound. Their bond had a depth and purity that Joy had not found elsewhere. "She understands *everything*," Joy wrote of Elsa in her diary.

Elsa's perceptiveness steadily grew. She knew the meaning of many words, such as *maji,* Swahili for water. She distinguished between human tones of firmness, frustration, and anger. She sensed who liked her, who tolerated her, and who was afraid of her—and, in a devilish mood, stalked or chased the frightened ones until

Joy or George yelled "STOP!" If she was excited or happy, she leaped toward Joy—yet, with great self-control, reined herself in at the last minute and landed at a safe distance from Joy's body. And if she was anxious or upset, she still came to suck Joy's thumbs.

Though Joy was opposed to killing animals, she knew Elsa needed meat in her diet; sheep or goats provided the food. But to keep Elsa from becoming too bloodthirsty at a young age and attacking donkeys and mules, until her second year Elsa was not shown animals being killed for food. If George shot a guinea hen for supper, Elsa carried it proudly to Joy as if it were a beautiful gift, not something to be devoured.

"We *must* teach Elsa to hunt," Joy finally said.

"But, Joy," George replied, "you know the limits of lions who are raised by people."

What Joy, George, and their crew would learn from Elsa and, later, from other lions that George raised, was that the current opinion about lions often was wrong. The lion, "king of beasts" feared in most cultures as powerful, fierce, and ruthless, is not only less likely to endanger humans than ethologists (scientists who study animal behavior) had thought, but is capable of creating with humans an abiding friendship and love. Joy and George kept rediscovering Elsa's loyalty. Her attachment to them never wavered, even when she showed signs of her natural, growing wildness—when shoulder bites she received on her solo outings indicated that she'd probably mated with a male lion, or when her not returning home for food showed that, contrary to opinion about domesticated lions, she'd probably hunted and killed on her own.

One afternoon, on a safari about four hundred miles from Isiolo, Joy, George, and Nuru found Elsa among the rapids of a tree-lined river. Soaked and panting, she was sitting on top of a buffalo that must have weighed twelve hundred pounds. They could see that the buffalo was old and guessed that Elsa had chased it into the river, where it slipped off the rocks among the rapids and she pushed its head under water. Injured and drowning, the buffalo was unable to defend itself against Elsa's attacks.

"George," Joy shouted, "please put the buffalo out of its misery!"

George took his gun from a side holster, aimed, and shot the buffalo in the head. Instantly, Nuru jumped into the water to cut the buffalo's throat before it died, an act required by his Muslim faith whenever meat from slaughtered animals was to be eaten. Elsa, however, her ears flattening, growled fiercely at Nuru. Though she accepted him as a trusted friend, she did not want him near her buffalo.

"No, no, no!" Nuru called, shaking his finger at Elsa. And, incredibly, she obeyed him, silencing her growls as Nuru slit the buffalo's throat. Moments later, while Joy, George, Nuru, and a few crew members waded through the rapids, puzzling over how to drag the huge animal to shore, Elsa suddenly decided to help. While Joy and the men pulled at the buffalo's head and legs, she jumped off its bleeding body, seized its tail, and pulled in unison alongside her human companions.

Back on land Joy and George hardly knew what to say to each other. In the flash of a moment, Elsa had squelched what was considered the strongest of her instincts—her need to guard her prey—in favor of her love for her family. Drenched and tired, licking Joy's arm, Elsa took one paw and hugged Joy to her wet body.

"Oh, George," Joy whispered hoarsely, "look at her! I love her so much, I'd be devastated without her—but she should have more than my love. I realize that no hand-reared lion has been successfully liberated to the wild, that they're killed by other lions for their ignorance of bush life. Yet, no matter what the risk, Elsa deserves to live free among her kind."

Taking Joy's hand, George nodded and turned toward the thickness of the African bush. Trees dripping with moss dotted the horizon. Sunlight streaked like arrows toward the ground. "Yes," George said, stroking Elsa's head. "Instead of someday sending her to a zoo or even to our Nairobi orphanage, we should offer Elsa her natural birthright."

CHAPTER 8

THE FIRST experiment began. Since Elsa could not roam free near Isiolo, which was too populated with tribespeople who would kill a stray lion, Joy and George received permission from officials to release her 350 miles away in an area filled with wild animals but uninhabited by people or livestock. When Joy was taking a series of poignant photographs on "leaving" day, Elsa, always camera shy, grabbed the camera with her teeth and bolted off with it. She eventually relinquished it, however; the camera was only slightly dented and the film safe.

In a Land Rover, Joy made Elsa as comfortable as possible in her traveling crate. When she and George crossed over the Great Rift Valley and reached their destination, they pitched camp eight thousand feet above sea level, overlooking a rolling plain. Below them were herds of Thomson's gazelles, roan antelope, rhinos, buffalo, Burchell's zebras, and wildebeests. Lions were also plentiful, providing possible companions and mates for Elsa. But neither Joy nor George had realized how the difference between Isiolo's semidesert climate and this colder, damper weather might affect Elsa. She shivered, plagued by rain that caused heavy mud in the waist-high grass.

At first Elsa rode on the roof of the Land Rover as she was introduced to her new surroundings. On nine or ten occasions, Joy and George searched for lions miles from camp, coaxed Elsa toward them into the bush, and—with Joy heartsick but hopeful—drove away without her. But when they returned in a few days, calling her name, she raced hysterically toward them, looking thin, dejected, and lonely. "We had . . . broken faith with her," Joy would write, "done so much to destroy her trust in us, yet she remained loyal." One evening, finding Elsa on a ridge where they'd left her days before, Joy saw the anguish on her face. "Indeed," Joy would write later, "she was nearly crying."

Joy and George made attempts to condition Elsa to her new home. Among the obstacles, however, was her fear of other lions. She greeted Joy with such tumultuous relief and desperation that Joy would temporarily allow her into the Land Rover. Once, Elsa found her own way back to camp, so glad to be there that she didn't stir when lions roared nearby. Smaller and darker than local lions, she'd begun to lose the shine on her coat. When rains flooded the area, she fell ill with swollen glands and fever. Joy treated her with a drug called M&B, and sent a crew member a hundred miles on foot with samples of Elsa's blood. The diagnosis was hookworm and tapeworm, complicated by a tick-borne virus. With Joy glued to her side, Elsa lay ill and in pain for five weeks, developing clusters of white hairs on her back. Finally she improved—but Joy called a halt to the experiment in the highlands.

A second attempt began in Meru Park, a hundred miles from Isiolo but only thirty-five miles from Elsa's birthplace in the Northern Frontier District. Here Elsa could thrive in her natural climate, with a hot sun, clumps of thornbush, and the Tana River, with its daily crowd of animals. On the red-tinged cliffs, Elsa could sit and survey the terrain or explore caves cut into the rock. Joy took her on two long walks a day, sometimes wanting to change any plans to liberate her. How strange it would feel, Joy thought, to walk alone with no lion brushing against her, no rough tongue licking her wrist. But, putting aside her longings, she always remembered how much Elsa deserved an independent life.

Soon Elsa was going off by herself again. Joy's wish was that a pride of lions at Meru Park—which protected its animals by not allowing hunting—would adopt Elsa, giving her a second family.

By month two of the Meru experiment, Joy was spending her afternoons at a log table she'd built under a tree at the river. Calling the spot her studio, she used it for writing and sketching, often with Elsa asleep at her feet. She'd sold a safari article to five European magazines, and the last 150 of her 560 tribal paintings had been purchased by the Kenyan government. Seventy paintings hung in the State House, not far from the Nairobi Museum's display of her renderings of a sunbird, crowned crane, hornbill, and chameleon. Now, following a new plan, she was putting Elsa's story down on paper. As she worked on an old, rusted typewriter, baboons gestured from across the lake, and bushbucks and lesser kudus walked by in graceful procession under a canopy of leaves. "I felt," Joy wrote, "as though I were on the doorstep of paradise: man and beast in trusting harmony; the slow-flowing river adding to the idyll."

If Joy or George went looking for Elsa, calling her or firing a shot in the air, they'd soon see her loping toward them, happier by far than during her first release. Exuberant, she might knock Joy down or put her whole mouth around Joy's head, but she quickly stopped her antics when scolded. If George took her fishing with him, she insisted on having the first fish caught on the hook—carrying it with dignity to his tent and dropping it on his bed. Elsa, Joy wrote, seemed to be saying, "This cold, strange kill is yours."

By November 1958 Elsa was spending many days and nights in the bush, obviously able—against all odds given by animal behaviorists—to survive. The experiment was succeeding, and there were signs that Elsa had mated with a male lion. Joy knew the time had come to break camp and, except for occasional visits, to leave Elsa behind. On November 13, in an open area at Meru called Elephant Lugga, Joy and George struggled to bid her good-bye. Kneeling on the dirt, Joy, now forty-eight years old, could no longer be stoic and hold back tears.

Throwing her arms around her "child," burying her face in the warm, golden fur, Joy moaned and trembled. Suddenly she heard a matching sound from Elsa's throat. She knew, then, from Elsa's response and from their embrace on the dirt, both the agony and beauty of a sacrifice made in the name of love. Rising to her feet, lurching away over the ground, she could barely follow George back to the Land Rover. She flung open the door, saw the tears on her husband's face, and threw herself onto the seat.

That night, while George sat in silent homage with his pipe, Joy nearly finished typing her story about Elsa. She held the flimsy, almost transparent pages against her chest, slowly turning to her open diary, and wondered where Elsa was in the darkness. Of their morning drive from camp to Elephant Lugga, Joy wrote, "[Elsa] knew everything and kept close to me on the way—leaving her for good. She licked and hugged me for the last time in my tears!"

The final "last time" still lay, for Joy and her lion, more than two years ahead. Each parting, however, held its deep grief and love; each embrace bruised yet strengthened the spirit.

IN FEBRUARY 1959, confident that Elsa could thrive with only sporadic visits from George, Joy went to England. She believed that Elsa's story must be published and had collected three albums of photographs to show with her manuscript. Renting a room in London near the well-known Harrods department store, she made the rounds of large publishing houses. None of them, however, wanted to publish a book about a lion.

Joy remembered a woman she'd met through Louis Leakey named Marjorie Villiers, cofounder of London's Harvill Press. Marjorie's partner, Manya Harari, had discovered and helped translate the great Russian novel *Doctor Zhivago*; both women owned dogs and were devoted to animals. Joy arrived at Harvill without an appointment and refused to leave the waiting room until Marjorie saw her. Their meeting, also attended by four poodles, stirred Marjorie to write an excited letter about "the lion book" to the chairman of Collins Publishers, the recent buyers of Harvill Press. The book's author, Marjorie said, was "this woman called Mrs. Adamson whose husband is a game warden [and who] has written a text of thirty thousand words." William (Billy) Collins was in New York on business when he received Marjorie's letter. Charming and flamboyant, he sent back a telegram: "Adamson book very exciting. Please arrange publish. No difficulty selling America."

Joy was offered a prepayment, or advance, of £1,000 (about $2,500), a good amount at the time. From Kenya, George agreed that letters he'd written to Joy about Elsa's progress could be included in the book—as long as readers were told that he had killed wild game for Elsa only if she needed it. Sitting each day with Harvill editors, Joy pored over her manuscript, improving the awkwardness of her English sentences, fighting to keep whatever material seemed crucial. Blue eyes flashing, chin thrust forward in stubbornness, she was as fearless at defending Elsa's story as she'd been at raising Elsa.

A former chief game warden of Uganda, C. R. S. Pitman, wrote a foreword to the book, and Lord William Percy of England, who had visited Joy in Kenya and befriended Elsa, wrote the preface. It was Percy who suggested the title *Born Free,* taken from Saint Paul's declaration in the Bible (Acts 22:28): "But I was free born." The book was published in 1960 by Collins in London and by Pantheon Books, a division of Random House, in the United States. Billy Collins arranged for posters and life-size replicas of Elsa in London bookstores, but even he was astounded by sales. Elsa, with her remarkable bonding to her foster parents and her pioneering return to the wild, captured the fancy of people everywhere. *Born Free* would, in time, sell six million copies, be translated into twenty-five languages, and have a readership of more than seventy million people. It inspired animal and science books and a hugely successful movie, sparked the founding of animal orphanages, charities, and refuge centers, and helped establish, in Africa and other countries, more national parks with laws against hunting. Its popularity ignited movements to protect endangered species, brought millions of tourists to Africa, and drew worldwide attention to Joy's tribal paintings.

"This book," said Peter Scott, an English naturalist and radio personality, "is in every sense a masterpiece. As a study of animal behavior it has a great importance;

as an example of near-perfect relationship between man and animal, it is unique."

When Joy returned to Kenya, she found her reunion with Elsa at Meru a true homecoming. Elsa was now fully wild in her living habits, but when she saw Joy, she retracted her claws and was as affectionate as ever. One problem arose, however, over a male lion brought to Meru by George to, perhaps, impregnate Elsa—something that had not occurred from any of her local matings. Unfortunately, the male lion killed six goats and seriously mauled two natives. Nearby tribesmen gathered up their spears, hatchets, and bush knives, cornered the lion, and hacked it to death. Writing to Marjorie Villiers, Joy described the event as a "nightmare." She felt partly responsible for the lion's "terrible end," and, ironically, Elsa soon mated with a local lion and became pregnant.

Elsa's cubs were due around Christmas. Though she was gaining weight, she still bounded out of the bush toward Joy and George whenever they visited her. They set up temporary camp with their crew, agreeing to use George's vacation time from his duties to stay at Meru through the end of Elsa's pregnancy. On Christmas morning Joy put out a silver tree sent from London by Marjorie Villiers, and at lunch she managed to eat the odd-tasting plum pudding that Kifosha, the cook, had, in ignorance, covered with Worcestershire sauce. Midway through the meal, Elsa arrived in a cloud of dust, meowing her hello, flipping cups off the table with her tail. Her stomach was no longer bulging; the sides of her body had slimmed. "Look!" Joy shouted. "She's announcing her cubs. What a gift for Christmas!"

Elsa kept coming alone to the camp for short periods. Joy and George were impatient to know how many cubs she'd delivered and if they were healthy, but by refusing to move if they tried to follow her, Elsa made it clear that she wanted no company in the bush. After New Year's, when Joy was temporarily in Isiolo, George looked on his own for the cubs. He climbed one of Elsa's favorite haunts, a tall rock formation he'd named Big Rock, quietly searching all sides.

As Joy returned to camp, George ran at her through the trees waving his hat in the air. She parked the Land Rover with a squeal of brakes and watched George hold up three fingers.

"What? What?" she yelled.

"Three!" he yelled back. "Elsa has three cubs!"

Crying in happiness, glad that George had tracked Elsa, Joy leaped from the Land Rover. She asked George breathless questions, then asked again. Where did he find the cubs? Did they seem safe from attack by other animals? Did Elsa know he'd discovered her lair? Was she angry? When did he think Elsa would allow anyone to see her babies? Were the cubs beautiful? Were they awake? Did they sense his presence?

"I found them alone in a cleft of rock," George answered. "They were awake, but, of course, their eyes are still closed."

Out of respect for Elsa, Joy did not try to see the

cubs. Elsa would visit camp, energetic and loving, then leave with an expression that seemed to say, "Sorry, but I have to go now. My children need me. I'm sure you understand."

It was a mid-February day when Joy and George, sitting in canvas folding chairs outside Kifosha's tent, noticed a shape swimming toward shore from the middle of the Tana River. They shielded their eyes from the sun and squinted at the river. "It's Elsa!" Joy said, then clutched George's sleeve. "But she's not alone! I can make out small movements behind her. Oh, the cubs; it's the cubs!"

And, indeed, Elsa had finally brought her babies to be viewed by her foster parents. Six weeks had passed since she'd given birth, enough time to be sure that the cubs had fully imprinted on Elsa, not on Joy or George. Again, Elsa had shown a perception and understanding that seemed human in scope.

Before long Elsa was standing on the banks of the Tana as her three children tumbled out of the waves. Shaking their small heads, wiggling their bodies in surprise at all the wetness, they stayed close to their mother. When they felt secure enough to roll over on the ground to dry themselves, their legs sticking upward, they looked like three cups of honey against the dark earth.

Joy was hesitant to move too close and frighten the cubs or upset Elsa. She remembered George rescuing Elsa and her baby sisters, bringing them to camp in his car. Now, with Elsa liberated from domesticity into the wild, her ability to live in two worlds—to partake fully in her natural environment yet maintain her loving bond with her human family—was extraordinary.

News of the cubs' birth had been wired to Collins Publishers and Pantheon Books. Newspapers and radio programs had picked up the story, carrying it across the world.

Sinking to her knees beside Elsa as the three cubs somersaulted over each other only a few feet away, Joy wanted to thank her beloved lion for bringing such treasures. "Your cubs," she whispered, her eyes moist once again, "are wonderful! Adventures await them, Elsa, in Meru Park—for they have what you had but almost lost: They are 'free born.'

"And," Joy added as she gazed intently into Elsa's eyes, "God willing, all of you will stay free."

CHAPTER 9

THOUSANDS OF letters addressed to Joy arrived in Isiolo from people who had read *Born Free* and heard news reports of the cubs' birth. Many wrote about coming to Kenya to see Joy, George, Elsa, and the cubs (who were named Jespah, Gopa, and Little Elsa). Though Joy did not want tourists to disturb Elsa, she had no legal means of barring them from Meru Park. She began to accept that she, George, and Elsa were celebrities; the *Illustrated London News* called Elsa a "world-famous lion," and two movie producers asked to film Elsa's story for the British Broadcasting Corporation (BBC). With her book royalties, Joy had already helped establish a new game post for preventing or catching poachers and had asked Meru's district commissioner how to develop another game reserve to protect animals.

At camp Elsa brought her cubs back and forth from the bush or river, disciplining them, cuddling them, showing them off. Joy tried not to tame them, but was irresistibly drawn to pet Little Elsa; lift Gopa, the timid one, onto her lap; or pull ticks from Jespah's tail. The cubs learned to drink from Elsa's old water bowl, a helmet cemented to a block of wood. If they playfully charged at Joy, they were stopped in their tracks by their mother.

Joy worried over the safety of her "brood." She hunted for poisonous snakes in camp and for the pale scorpions whose sting caused convulsions. One morning Elsa appeared with a torn and bleeding ear, probably from an attack by another lion. But the most anxious time was the spring of 1960, when a grass fire swept the area, burning the camp tents and covering everyone with ash. After the fire, Elsa and the cubs nonchalantly appeared, unharmed, among the ruins.

Billy Collins visited Joy and Elsa, eager to discuss a world tour for Joy and a sequel to *Born Free*. Another visitor was Sir Julian Huxley, a famous biologist and author who had been director general of UNESCO, the United Nations Educational, Scientific, and Cultural Organization. Sir Julian stayed in his car if Elsa was nearby, but Billy, never to be daunted, slept in one of the scorched tents. Though Elsa welcomed him by jumping on his cot, nibbling at his arm, and holding his cheeks with her teeth, he was remarkably calm and gentle toward her.

In May, Joy and George planned to leave camp for Isiolo. They postponed departure, however, when rumors flew that Elsa might be killed by poachers from the Tharaka tribe who were angry over the new game post, or by herdsmen who were afraid to graze cattle in Elsa's territory. (Some Tharakas and other Kenyan tribespeople were killing fewer animals because they realized wildlife was often an asset for farming, tourism, and employment.)

Toward December, rumors about Elsa's enemies grew louder. Her fame caused hostility from poachers who'd been arrested by George at Meru. Stories also circulated about a lion who had killed two men. While no one had identified the lion, Elsa was blamed. On Christmas Day, with memories strong of the prior Christmas season, when Elsa had given birth, Joy stacked presents on a wreath of tinsel. Elsa and the cubs joined the festivities, with Jespah chewing up George's gift-wrapped shirt. Joy and George opened sacks of mail. Among holiday cards from friends, family, and well-wishers was a single letter sent from the district commissioner. "Mercifully," Joy said, "it was one of the last envelopes I opened. It contained an order for the removal of Elsa and her cubs from the reserve."

Though the official letter spoke of everyone's best interests, Joy was stunned. Elsa had lived in Meru Park for two and a half years; now she had to be uprooted. George suggested moving her and the cubs to the Lake Rudolph area, but Joy had found it too grim and depressing for a permanent habitat. While the saddened crew built a ramp to coax the lions into a government truck, Joy wrote to friends in Tanganyika (now Tanzania), Uganda, and Rhodesia (now Rwanda), asking advice about a new home for Elsa. But before any decision was made, Joy noticed that Elsa was scratching at maggot bites which had become infected. Her nose was wet and cold to the touch, often a sign of illness, and she refused to let Joy dress her sores.

Arrangements had been made for Joy to fly to Nairobi to discuss Elsa and the cubs with Ian Grimwood, chief game warden, but she wouldn't leave until she felt sure that Elsa was better. Rubbing against Joy's hip, Elsa said her own "thank you" for the fresh meat Joy had left for her on the riverbank. She carried it up a slope to her cubs and turned to look back at Joy with a wag of her tail.

In Nairobi Joy's ears rang from the sharp city noises as she walked to her appointment with Ian, yet before she could sit down in his office, she was handed a telegram wired through Isiolo. "Elsa worse," George had written. "Has high fever. Suggest bring aureomycin."

The first flight from Nairobi was not until the following day. By morning one of George's friends, Ken Smith, had driven 180 miles to give Joy a second message: Elsa was desperately ill. George had found her sprawled weakly under a tree while the cubs sat nearby. He had brought her water and meat mixed with medicine, but she could neither eat nor drink. Alarmed, not knowing why she was so sick, he spent the night in the bush beside her.

As Joy and Ken learned later, Elsa made one immense, valiant effort that night to rise to greet George, but she collapsed at his feet. At dawn George and Nuru brought her into camp on a stretcher they'd made from a cot and wooden poles. She lay mutely in George's tent, gazing at him, once summoning up enough strength to drag herself in obvious torture to the river. She still could not drink, however, and even the milk and whiskey George squirted into her mouth by syringe dribbled away. Though he tried to stop her, she stumbled bravely to a thicket where she'd often played with the cubs. Her breath was labored as she fell onto the sodden mud, the cubs pacing in bewilderment around her. George tried moving her to dry sand, but she was suddenly beyond making any physical effort. He held her head in his lap, his eyes streaming with tears. He would describe her agony as a "terrible, harrowing sight."

When Joy and Ken arrived by plane at the nearest Somali village, they drove the last seventy miles into camp at high speed. Racing onto the campsite, propelled by a terrifying urgency, Joy found George alone in a canvas chair. He looked at her with devastating sorrow. She knew at once what she could not bear to hear.

"She's gone, Joy," George said. "I have no reasons. Jespah licked her face at the end—and she gave a heart-rending cry as she left us. I believe she was telling you good-bye."

Joy stood frozen in the blast of African sun. *What, dear God,* she asked, *had happened?* How could Elsa, who now would never have to leave Meru but whose love had been the pure grace of Joy's life, ever have died without her?

GEORGE HAD ALREADY buried Elsa, wanting to spare Joy the sight of the body, which had been cut open to remove some organs for autopsy. At the grave, marked by George with a mound of stones as a memorial, Joy sank to her knees. It seemed to her that Elsa had been alive for only a moment, like the white blossoms on a tree that grows in Kenya, the *Sesamnothamnus busseanus,* which live for just a night. She knew that the normal lifespan of a lion was twelve to fifteen years; Elsa had died at the age of five. The autopsy results, which Joy went to pick up in Nairobi, showed a tick-borne virus, *Babesia,* that destroyed Elsa's red corpuscles. It had never before been identified in a lion.

In her despair, Joy stumbled over a tree stump at camp and fell, gashing her leg so badly it had to be treated in a hospital and rebandaged every day for a month.

Elsa's death had been reported across the world, bringing thousands of sympathy telegrams to Isiolo. But as much as Joy and George needed to recuperate from their grief, they still felt responsible for Elsa's cubs. Jespah, Gopa, and Little Elsa had fled into the bush after their mother's death, and were reported to have mauled, or perhaps killed, some cows and goats of Tharaka tribesmen. George paid the Tharakas for their losses while he and Joy searched for the cubs. Writing to Marjorie Villiers, Joy said, "I promise I will try to get the cubs through, unless anything happens to me. Then there will be George—he must always have access to money . . . to help the cubs."

Local and foreign newspapers picked up the story of the injured cows and goats, printing headlines such as ELSA'S CUBS MAY HAVE TO BE SHOT, DEATH THREATS

TO ELSA'S CUBS, ELSA'S CUBS: SENTENCE OF DEATH. To save the sixteen-month-old cubs from the Tharakas, Joy and George requested and received permission to transport them to Serengeti National Park in Tanganyika (now Tanzania), six hundred miles away. Without adequate time for his job, and with the difficult task ahead of catching the cubs, moving them, and monitoring their safety until they were either accepted or killed by animals in the Serengeti, George—at age fifty-five—retired on April 23, 1961, from his post as game warden, which he had held for twenty-five years.

Luring the cubs into camp was a long, frustrating chore. Joy's leg wound was still oozing, the crew had malaria and dysentery, and a flood raged over the camp, destroying supplies. George and the crew finally baited three heavy crates with goat meat and lifted them onto a truck with ropes and pulleys. When the cubs returned to camp, they raided the crates and were trapped by the falling doors. Sadly, Joy and George began the arduous three-day drive to the Serengeti. They felt deeply pained by the sight of the caged cubs. Heavy rains, icy winds, and choking dust sent Jespah, dejected and confused, into the back of his crate, while Gopa and Little Elsa, looking numb with fright, were thrown against the metal caging as the truck hit ruts in the dirt. When Joy tried to clean out the urine and feces in the crates, she had to fight swarms of bluebottle flies. As the cubs, too, were attacked by the insects, they desperately used their paws to hide their faces.

In the Serengeti, bruised and dirty from their ride,

the cubs were released in a valley forty miles long. Local officials knew that Joy and George would not kill game for the cubs within the reserve, but still insisted that the Adamsons could camp there only a month. Joy and George slept in the truck, with an oil lamp left burning all night and fresh meat laid out for the cubs. In daylight, worried over their safety, Joy decided to search for them by herself. She could not find them, however, in the thick brambles. By month's end, with the grass too high to track spoor and not knowing if the cubs had learned to feed themselves, she managed to convince officials to grant camping privileges for another week. On the last day, Jespah, Gopa, and Little Elsa finally ran up to the truck, swallowed cod liver oil from Joy's hand, but refused food. "They're eating on their own!" Joy said. "Their bellies look full!"

"We'll leave now," George replied, snapping some photos. "We'll visit them. We know we've tended to Elsa's children."

Outside the Serengeti, Billy Collins flew in from London to console Joy over Elsa's death and to plan her world tour. He suggested that Joy show audiences a film of Elsa that she and George had shot.

Together, Joy, George, and Billy witnessed, in awe, the vast yearly migration of animals to Lake Victoria. Stretching for miles, columns of animals came to the lake's plentiful water supply when other water holes had dried up in the heat. There were so many animals that the ground itself seemed to be moving. The migration contained, in one year's survey, 500,000 Thomson's gazelles, 221,699 wildebeests, 151,006 zebras, 15,898 buffalo, 15,766 topi, 2,450 eland, 1,379 kongoni, 720 elephants, 400 lions, and 29 rhinos.

Before Joy left on her tour, she launched Elsa Wild Animal Appeal in Africa, a charity to help animals living where they were unwanted by human beings; she also set up the Nature Conservancy Committee to issue grants from her royalties. She hired an animal rescue team and bought them a truck, which was painted with the name ELSA LIMITED.

Through her last year with Elsa, Joy had not stopped writing, taking photographs, or painting. She'd produced *Elsa,* a collection of photographs and text for children; *Living Free,* the sequel to *Born Free* and already a top seller at Collins Publishers; and a third volume, about Elsa's cubs, *Forever Free,* being edited by Marjorie Villiers. Billy Collins, convalescing from a tsetse fly bite that had caused a blood clot, promised to publish another book she was finishing, full of her photos and paintings of African tribes.

Joy's first public appearance, before an audience of three thousand, was in September 1962, in London. She hoped to raise money for Elsa Appeal, but the prospect of sounding strange with her Austrian accent and awkward English felt more chilling to her than being chased by stampeding elephants. She was so anxious that she vomited before her appearance and cried when she spoke of Elsa. In other cities she taught herself to stand rigidly during her talks and shielded herself from questions about Elsa's death. Her tour took her across the world—to South Africa, where Ziebel, her first husband, asked for her autograph in a Cape Town bookstore, to India, Thailand, Singapore, New Zealand, Australia, Europe, and the United States. She was often booked for three talks a day, sometimes in different cities. She wrote later, "Often I walked onto the platform not knowing how I would start, let alone get through the lecture. Yet once I faced that audience it was as if my talk were dictated by an unknown power."

With copies of *Born Free* and *Living Free* stacked nearby, she spoke of returning Elsa to the wild. She described the great wonder of the animal kingdom, the need for contributions for more reserves, national parks, and benevolent zoos, and for rescuing animals in peril. Elsa, she explained, might have been sent to George and her as a reminder to the world that people are part of nature and should live "in harmony with other creatures." In writing *Born Free,* she said, she'd hoped readers would understand that animals are not ordinary, dumb, or inferior, but are magnificent, intelligent, and wise. The human species, she added, must struggle not only for its own survival but also for the survival of mammals, birds, and reptiles, both wild and domestic; otherwise, the future is jeopardized for all.

Joy appeared at Holloway Prison (for women) in London, speaking from the pulpit of the chapel to a large crowd of inmates. The severest criminals were seated in the back rows; shoplifters, prostitutes, and other petty offenders filled the front seats. Before she could say anything, Joy heard loud catcalls and swear words flying at her in disdain. She was startled, but she just smiled. *Come on, Elsa,* she thought, *we'll do this together.*

Looking into the eyes of the inmates, Joy began talking. As she told the story of Elsa and the cubs, of what life had been in the African wild, of what she desired for orphaned, abused, neglected, sick, or unwanted animals everywhere, she felt as if Elsa's face were rubbing again across her hip, the unbroken bond between them transcending the boundaries of life and death.

At the end of her speech, Joy stretched out her arms toward her female audience. Cheers and applause broke through the silence. Inmates, even the most hardened, were able to open their hearts to the animal world. Jumping up onto their seats, they waved and clapped and emptied their pockets of the few coins they were allowed for their only store-bought pleasures: cigarettes and candy. About thirty inmates, their faces tear-streaked, put coins for Elsa Appeal in a bowl at Joy's feet. Some began a chant as they drummed their fists on the wooden backs of the chairs. "Elsa! Elsa! Elsa!" they called.

As Joy left Holloway Prison, the chants of the inmates went with her into the misty London streets. There, like a chain of honor, they joined inseparably and lovingly with her own incantation of Elsa's name.

CHAPTER 10

RETURNING TO Kenya was a longing made real. On tour in New York, Joy had been unable to "glimpse the sky above the concrete chasms of...skycrapers." In Kenya she found a stillness broken mainly by the call of animals, and a "sense of immensity" that could dissolve everyday concerns.

Yet, in 1964, Kenya's stillness was interrupted on a seven-hundred-acre farm at the foot of Mount Kenya. A movie contract for *Born Free* had been signed with California's Columbia Pictures. Twenty-four lions and an elephant were brought in from U.S. zoos, as well as a director and a producer, a crew of technicians and their equipment, dozens of African workers, and enough huts to form a small village. Joy was asked to live on the farm to brief the press and make certain the animals were well treated. She and George would be played in the movie by Hollywood stars Virginia McKenna and Bill Travers. To Joy's relief, the couple—married to each other—

refused to work with the two trained circus lions supposed to represent Elsa. They insisted on a more natural, authentic bond with a lion, and took eight weeks before filming to make friends, through George's guidance, with two half-grown lions, Boy and Girl.

Whenever George was tired and lay in the farm grass, Girl stalked him, jumped on his back, and bit his neck. What could have been deadly, however, stayed calm. Girl squelched her aggressiveness and, trusting George, would sit down, waiting to be petted. On the days the movie needed a beginning-attack scene, George simply lay on his stomach near Girl.

The filming of *Born Free,* the first movie to depict such a deep bond between human beings and a wild animal, was completed in 1965. To mark the occasion, Joy took Virginia McKenna on a visit to Elsa's grave in Meru Park. With donations from Joy's trust, now set up in London, Meru operated as a national reserve. Using Joy's written suggestions, the Kenyan government was developing further plans to help preserve the country's wildlife. Kenya itself, along with other African colonies, had been granted *uhuru,* or independence, by Great Britain. Its prime minister, now freed from jail, was Jomo Kenyatta.

After the *Born Free* film crew left Africa, Joy was booked on another tour, this time to promote "Elsa's movie." She was presented to Queen Elizabeth at a Royal Command Performance of *Born Free* in London and attended openings in New York, Washington, Boston, and San Francisco. *Born Free* became a box office hit all over the world and won an Academy Award for its music.

Before the tour Joy had been given a female cheetah by an army officer's family that was moving and couldn't take their pet with them. Joy had named the cheetah Pippa and slowly liberated it to Meru Park, where she began a study of its habits. When she traveled to London, she left George at Meru to help Pippa, if needed, with birthing her first cubs. "Little did I know," Joy wrote after the premiere, "that, perhaps at the very moment in which the Scots Guards heralded the Queen's arrival with all the traditional splendor and I was being presented to Her Majesty, alone, deep in Kenya's bush, Pippa was giving birth to three free-born children. This was the culmination of all that *Born Free* meant to me."

Pippa eventually had four litters of cubs, but two of the litters were killed by animals. Joy kept close track of the survivors, bringing them food and water in case Pippa had difficulty managing the task.

Joy wrote two books about Pippa and her children, *The Spotted Sphinx* and *Pippa's Challenge*. Her books provided scientists with new information about cheetahs. Once the royal pets of Genghis Khan, the Mongol conqueror, and of Charlemagne, the emperor of western Europe in the Middle Ages, cheetahs are totally different in nature from lions. Solitary and shy, keeping out of sight, they are the fastest of all mammals, topping by twenty to thirty miles the forty-mile-per-hour speed of racehorses. Joy observed the love play of Pippa's maturing cubs with other cheetahs, took photographs, described their ritualized behavior, and showed that cheetahs, like lions, communicate with each other across many miles.

While Joy stayed with Pippa at Meru, George set up camp twelve miles away with three lions from the *Born Free* movie—Girl, Boy, and Ugas. The two camps were separated because cheetahs and lions are natural enemies. The distance made for loneliness, but Joy and George tolerated it. They still argued over Joy's moodiness or George's silence, and both of them had occasionally been unfaithful—Joy with Billy Collins when he'd visited Kenya, and George with several native women. But neither argument nor infidelity could destroy their relationship. George never stopped loving Joy, and she, though still wary of human closeness, would drop everything and rush to George's rescue if he was in need.

In 1966 the director of Kenya's national parks asked Joy if she would raise and release two orphaned leopard cubs. Though leopards are considered the most dangerous of Africa's animals, Joy accepted the challenge. Driving to pick up the cubs, however, she skidded on a steep slope, hit a marker embedded in the dirt, and lost consciousness as the Land Rover tumbled down a jagged incline. When she awakened, she was lying on the ground on splintered glass; the Land Rover had missed plunging into the Tana River only because it caught on some bushes. Bruised and shaken, she looked at her right hand: It was an almost unrecognizable lump of torn flesh, blood, and dirt.

Joy crawled up the slope, her hand throbbing with excruciating pain, and collapsed at the road. She was found by a group of Africans and by George's assistant, Tony Baxendale, who happened by. Tony drove her to the hospital at Embu, eighty miles away, where a skin patch from her leg was grafted onto the back of her hand. Her injury was so severe, she had to wait six months for some healing to take place before the severed tendons and broken bones could be treated. In all, she endured six major operations on her hand, one of them in London, yet regained only the use of her thumb and, partially, her index finger. Never again could she tackle the rigors of safari—or draw, paint, or play the piano—with her usual skill. Yet her defiance did not leave her; in the hospital she asked George for a typewriter and taught herself to type with her left hand.

In 1969, while recovering from her London surgery, Joy heard from a nurse that an exhibition of her tribal paintings had opened nearby. She went to the London gallery, gratified at the size of the crowd but surprised that, alongside twenty of her original paintings loaned from the Nairobi Museum, fifty-six reproductions of her work were offered for sale. She demanded to know how the man who'd arranged the exhibition had obtained permission to make reproductions.

"Oh," the man answered haughtily, "the trustees of Nairobi Museum let me reproduce some of your portraits. This exhibition, Mrs. Adamson, is traveling across the world. All sales will be split between the museum and myself."

Over the more than six years Joy had spent painting the seven hundred tribal portraits, her government commission hardly covered expenses. Honors had come, including the recent news that Jomo Kenyatta had hung three hundred of what he called her "historic paintings" in Kenya's State House. But standing in the London gallery, her bandaged right hand held stiffly against her chest, Joy realized with dismay that not only had the museum not asked her about reproductions nor paid her for this traveling exhibition, but she would be charged like a customer off the street for any prints of her work she might like to take home.

"The civilized world," Joy said to the snide, gray-suited man in the gallery, "is far more savage than any African jungle."

TIME, JOY NOTICED, was slipping away. Her body, having served her well in a rugged life, seemed, at age fifty-five, less resilient. Aside from her damaged hand, she had developed arthritis, pain in her neck and hip, recurring malaria, a fluttering heartbeat, and kidney stones. In falls on lava and rock, she had broken her right elbow and fractured her right knee. Thinking ahead, she hoped for a place where she and George might live comfortably in their later years, and she found it on Lake Naivasha, about a hundred miles from Isiolo. Hidden from the road was a stone house on fifty acres of waterfront, overlooking sprays of pink water lilies and soft cushions of moss. Antelope, otters, spring hare, bushbucks, colobus monkeys, and long-tailed mongooses wandered the property. Hippos came at night to munch noisily on the grass. Beyond a line of yellow fever trees on the hills, lions, giraffes, buffalo, and zebras lived. Using money from her trust, Joy bought the house, naming it Elsamere.

George built an extra bungalow at Elsamere and an outdoor wire enclosure for sick or injured animals. Joy brought her favorite mementos from Isiolo and unpacked her German books on spirituality to start a small library. A few windows were enlarged to bring in more light, and Joy's piano—though she could no longer play it—was placed in the main room.

Elsamere kept Joy busier than usual, a balm for her emotions. Yet in 1969, eight years after Elsa's death, Pippa suddenly died.

Joy discovered Pippa within three hundred yards of camp at Meru, thin, hungry, and dragging a broken foreleg. By the looks of her, the cheetah had limped for miles to reach Joy. When a vet was flown in from Nairobi, he found Pippa's foreleg fracture so extensive that he advised putting her to sleep. Flatly refusing, Joy had Pippa flown to the Nairobi animal hospital. For eighteen days she stayed by Pippa's side, sleeping next to her at night. The leg wound, however, developed gangrene, and heavy sedatives caused Pippa's heart to fail. Tenderly helping lift her onto dry ice, Joy drove Pippa home to burial at Meru.

Periodically Joy hiked over rugged terrain to track Pippa's children. One of them, Whity, never stopped recognizing her, coming within inches to drink water from a bowl. Joy would visit Elsa's and Pippa's graves, leaving flowers, washing the stones, smoothing the ground. At Elsa's grave, as if her lion child was still soothing her, Joy always felt a rare sense of peace. The trust shown her by Elsa and by most of the animals she'd rescued was what she had longed for at Seifenmühle when she'd talked of animals with her cousin Peter.

Joy's work with animals enlightened the millions of people who read her books. Though her goal never was money, her earnings from three adult Elsa books, several spin-off productions, and the movie *Born Free* were £250,000, which, in today's inflated dollars, would equal almost $4,000,000. She kept little of the money for herself, but sent most of it to her trust to aid her favorite causes. She accepted invitations to speak in the U.S.S.R., Japan, Hungary, and Thailand (where, by coincidence, the *Born Free* movie was showing in Bangkok); she scheduled press conferences and visited animal research stations, breeding farms, and zoos. Talking to people whenever possible of the "disastrous plight" of endangered species—cheetahs, pandas, mountain gorillas, Japanese cranes, Przewalski's horses—she financed animal rescue teams in Russia, Poland, Czechoslovakia, Hungary, Romania, and Bulgaria.

The Elsa Wild Animal Appeal, which Joy mentioned at every press conference, opened offices in England and Canada and, under the name Elsa's Nature Conservancy, in Japan. Thirty-seven Elsa Clubs operated in the United States, all promoting wildlife conservation and helping to establish game reserves and national parks. School-children in many countries raised money for the Appeal through cake sales and raffles.

In 1973 Joy's mother died. Though she had never regained her early closeness with her mother, Joy had been sending her money. Now any chance for further reunion was gone. A few years later, in 1976, Billy Collins died. His intelligence and charm had fascinated Joy, and his death marked the end of a seventeen-year friend-ship during which he had published ten books she'd written—seven for adults (including *Joy Adamson's Africa*) and three for children.

At the time Collins died Joy was working on her own autobiography, *The Searching Spirit*. Begun in the mid-1970s and published in 1978, it covers her years in Austria and Africa, with great emphasis on her relationships with Elsa, Pippa, and other animals. Before its publication, she was consulted by Bill Travers and his associate, James Hill, on a film about her and George, but an argument with Bill turned her against the project. The film, called *The Lions Are Free,* was made without her participation and was shown on NBC and CBS television in the United States, prompting thousands of letters from children wanting to tame lions or become game wardens. In England a TV documentary, made with Joy's assistance and photos, showed Pippa at Meru Park, while an American TV series starring Diana Muldaur and Gary Collins was loosely based on *Born Free.*

On Joy's visit to the U.S.S.R., she had been invited to make a graft on the famous Friendship Tree, a citrus planted in 1934 at the seaside resort of Sochi. Many renowned people representing 126 countries had made nearly 150 grafts on the tree with cuttings from other fruit trees, each graft marked with a name and date on a ceramic tag. Grafts had honored such luminaries as Louis Pasteur, Van Cliburn, and Charles Darwin, and soil from the graves of Mahatma Gandhi, Leo Tolstoy, Alexander Pushkin, and Peter Ilich Tchaikovsky circled the base of the tree.

Standing beside the Friendship Tree, wind from the Black Sea ruffling her blouse, Joy held a cutting from an orange tree, a pair of garden scissors, and a twelve-inch length of grafting twine. Speaking in German and English to a small crowd, she said, "I make this graft in the name of Elsa the lion, from whose example we have learned so much about the nobility of animals."

Joy snipped off the end of a thin branch on the tree and fit her cutting there, slowly winding the grafting twine around the two pieces. An official stepped forward to place soft sealing wax across the twine. Turning to a white-haired woman beside her, Joy said, "The two branches are joined as Elsa and I were joined. What could be more beautiful?"

Nodding, the woman touched the bark of the tree. "When people learn," she answered, "that *all* creatures are united in their gift of life, peace may come at last to the earth."

"And then," Joy said, reciting from Isaiah, as she

recalled her childhood dream of living among the animals, " 'the wolf shall dwell with the lamb, and the leopard shall lie down with the kid; the calf and the lion and the sheep shall abide together, and a little child shall lead them.' "

CHAPTER 11

DAYS AT Elsamere turned, for Joy, like pages of books she'd written, one leading in anticipation to the next. George was often sixty miles away, raising and liberating lions at a camp he'd built at Kora, an area dense with rock and thornbush. When Boy was injured, George brought him to recuperate in Elsamere's animal enclosure, but the rest of his fourteen lions stayed behind. Joy walked in the hills to gain strength as she recovered from surgery to replace an arthritic hip with a steel implant. She photographed colobus monkeys, their black-and-white capes of hair billowing like clouds as they jumped through the trees, and Verreaux's eagle owls, whose golf ball–size eyes stared at her from under pink eyelids fringed with white lashes. She rescued a young eagle owl suffering from a broken wing and confined it to the enclosure until the visiting vet, who had given it an injection, said it could fly.

Joy wrote down her tales of monkeys and owls,

which were published as *Friends from the Forest*. Some afternoons she sat on a grassy edge of Lake Naivasha, listening to recorded tapes of Mozart, Schubert, Chopin, and Brahms. The mail kept flowing into Elsamere, and friends paid visits. Joy often invited guests she'd met in Africa and abroad to dinner. She entertained scientists, environmentalists, reporters, movie stars, filmmakers, and politicians. Invariably the talk concerned her work. "Elsa," she told guests, "was not an exception among lions. The species has a far wider range of response than scientists have believed. Many of our beliefs lead to ignorance, chaos, violence, and war."

In November 1976 Joy was given an abandoned two-month-old female leopard, her first chance to raise a leopard since her hand injury. She named the cub Penny and kept her in an enclosure, often writing beside her. Colobus monkeys pounced on the cage to tease the new resident, learning to avoid her claws. Though Penny bonded to Joy, she had to be controlled on walks by a long metal leash and was more ferocious than Elsa or most of George's lions. She did not retract her claws during play and, after having many stitches for scratches or bites, Joy ordered a canvas apron, gauntlets, and leg guards. She was fascinated by Penny and planned to study her behavior. "I can see in her eyes," Joy wrote, "the deep, unfathomable conflict between love and the ability to murder."

Joy received permission from Kenya's Wildlife Department to begin Penny's release in Shaba, a nearby reserve of a hundred square miles. Taking six workers and an assistant with her, including her old cook, Kifosha, Joy set up camp. Knowing that leopards move out of set boundaries, she asked the vet to fit Penny with a tracking collar that would transmit signals for four miles on land and forty miles by air. If Penny wasn't seen for a week, Joy could track her in a small rented plane.

At Shaba Penny learned to drag a dead animal of her own weight up a tree to store it in the fork of two limbs. Watching her adjust to the freedom of the bush, Joy began a book about her called *Queen of Shaba*. In February 1979 she saw mating bites on Penny's shoulder, and in May wrote Marjorie Villiers that two cubs had been born on "a large rocky outcrop of forbidding cliffs, precipices, boulders, and loose stone." Surprisingly, Penny left the cubs alone to lead Joy and her crew to see the babies. A few days later, however, she became secretive. "She looked at [the cubs] so tenderly," Joy wrote. "It was unbelievable how she...[was now changing] into the role of a mother. [As]...the little ones snuggled between her front feet, she licked our hands and allowed us to stroke her, all so peaceful and happy—except when a hawk flew over us and Penny's eyes narrowed and followed it with a murderous expression."

The birth of Penny's cubs gave Joy a sense of renewal. Though hospitalized for a liver swollen from malaria and typhoid, she wrote with bravado to George: "I am now 68 and wish I could have fifty years to do all I would like to do. Apart from a steel hip, a broken hand, elbow, knee and ankle—all on the right side...I am very fit (touch wood). I can stumble for hours across wobbling lava in the heat and drench myself, fully dressed, several times a day under the shower to keep mentally active."

In 1977, at a ceremony held by the Austrian Ambassador to Kenya, Joy was awarded the Austrian Cross of Honor for Science and Arts. The greatest tribute of its kind her homeland could bestow, the cross was a momentous achievement for the woman who'd once been little Friederike Gessner, an Austrian girl who'd left sad poems on her mother's pillow. She still, however, had feelings of being betrayed by people. Back at Elsamere, having put the cross in the library for George to see, Joy fired some of her small staff of hired workers—gardeners, house servants, drivers, night watchmen. Some were let go for alcoholism or theft, but others were unfairly dismissed.

Every sundown, with no weapon to protect her, Joy walked in the bush, a longtime practice that worried her friends. She liked feeling alone with nature. She could test herself against the perils of unarmed solitude, and on those occasions when a rhino charged through the bush, a poisonous snake hissed its menace, or a crocodile opened its jaws, she escaped without gun or spear, ignoring scuffed knees, branch cuts on her cheek, or the heaving of her chest from a run for her life. In her bedroom she'd listen to the seven o'clock news on a scratched radio, letting civilization seep slowly into her mind.

But on January 3, 1980, after Joy returned from a trip to Paris—where the *Born Free* movie had been shown on TV and she had sat on a discussion panel with movie star

Brigitte Bardot and other animal lovers—her walk in the bush seemed unsettling. Years of tracking spoor or sensing the presence of human beings from the noise of a cracking branch, or the barest outline of feet upon fallen leaves, or a certain dank odor, alerted Joy to possible danger. On that January evening, as she strolled among six-foot-high reeds, she paused to hear or see what it was she sensed. Suddenly a slim, dark figure pushed forward, and she recognized a worker, Paul Ekai, who'd been fired for breaking into her trunk and stealing money. About nineteen years old, a member of the Turkana tribe, he'd been angry at his dismissal; she remembered the vein pulsing on his forehead the night he had fled Elsamere. "Paul," she said, "Why are you here?"

"You owe me back pay," he answered, half in English and half in Swahili.

Joy felt her own anger rippling through her. "I already paid you enough wages," she said. "I owe you *nothing*. You're a thief! You stole money."

"You owe me," he said again.

"Go away at once, or I'll notify the police," Joy told him. "You'd already be in jail if we had known where to find you."

In a slash of Paul Ekai's hand, Joy felt a burning in her ribs that almost extinguished her breath. Unable to speak, she fell onto the path. Dirt filled her mouth as she tried to resist, but in the throbbing heat of the bush, her shock gave way to darkness. No stranger, the darkness had greeted her thousands of times in her years in Africa, had taken Elsa, Pati, Pippa, and so many others. Now, unexpectedly, she herself traveled into this mysterious dark. Blood seeped from her, but she felt no regrets. She had always chosen risk over safety. She would not, even now, be victim to fear. Lying among the reeds and the blood, she showed the same grit and courage she had shown all her life—even as Paul Ekai ended, with murder, the final chapter of her sixty-ninth year.

JOY'S ASSISTANT, Pieter Mawson, went looking for Joy when she didn't return for the evening news broadcast, and he found her body on the path, a large wound on her left arm. He thought a lion had killed her. Lifting her into a station wagon, Pieter drove back to Elsamere to tell Kifosha, the cook, of the ghastly circumstances. He continued on to the local doctor's house at Isiolo, taking the doctor in the car with Joy to the police station. Two hours later, Joy's body was transported to the hospital mortuary at Meru.

George, informed by police of her death, was totally disconsolate but refused to believe a lion was responsible. "Joy didn't die that way," he said.

Newspapers everywhere reported Joy's death, bringing a deluge of telegrams and letters to George at Kora, to Elsamere, and to Collins Publishers. Peter Bally, now eighty-five years old, flew in to pay his respects to his ex-wife at the mortuary, commenting after seeing her that Joy had never lost her beauty. Ziebel von Klarwill wrote two of her friends, expressing his love for the woman he'd married forty-five years earlier. Joy's funeral was held at the crematorium in Nairobi, attended by

Austrian, English, and Kenyan mourners—friends, relatives, and ardent members of animal rescue groups. Her ashes, as directed in her will, were buried in the soil of Elsa's and Pippa's graves, and George ordered a metal plaque to mark the path where she was killed.

When an autopsy proved that Joy had died from human, not animal, assault—a puncture wound, probably from a *simi* knife, was in her ribcage and had at first gone undetected—Paul Ekai and a few other former workers at Elsamere were put on a "wanted" list. On February 2, two hundred miles away at Baragoi, Paul Ekai was arrested and confessed to killing Joy. He led police to his discarded *simi,* handing over a bag of clothes stolen from Pieter Mawson and a torch taken from Elsamere. Medical examiners in Nairobi tested bloodstains on the bag and matched them to Joy's blood type.

Though Paul Ekai withdrew his confession, causing unfounded rumors about Pieter Mawson's role in Joy's death, he was convicted of murder on October 28, 1981. He was sentenced to prison. Had he been older, a full adult, he would have been put to death. An appeal from his lawyer failed when three judges, considering the evidence, upheld the conviction on December 14, 1981. Shortly afterward, Pieter Mawson was killed in a car accident; of other workers Joy had hired at Elsamere, only Kifosha kept in contact with George.

In articles and books that have been written about Joy, she emerges as uniquely gifted, intense, and powerfully brave, a woman who tossed off danger like a trifle or embraced it like a friend. Millions of readers have learned of her tribal paintings gracing private and government collections, and of her remarkable botanical drawings. They read of her beloved lion, her high-spirited cheetah, her ferocious leopard, all successfully returned to the wild. They "heard," in her quoted words, her pleas to mankind to question its harshness and arrogance. "Humans," Joy wrote in *The Spotted Sphinx*, "are the most highly evolved and intellectually advanced of species, yet we are the only ones who ruthlessly violate the balance of nature by directing our achievements mainly to our own benefit. We look to destroy anything which may look to us as if it competes with our own convenience." Animals, Joy declared, can teach us, guide us, and help tame our need to control.

Though Joy's will provided George with £8,000 per year (about $78,000 in today's dollars), Elsa Appeal received the majority of her estate. Joy had helped establish four national parks in Kenya—Meru, Shaba, Samburu, and Hell's Gate—and a number of wildlife clubs. Canada's Elsa Appeal initiated owl research and built a rehabilitation center near Niagara to study fourteen Canadian owl species. Other Appeal projects included supporting government legislation to ban the leg-hold trap and aiding forest preserves with a humane deer management program.

Knowledge of Joy and her work was one of the reasons for heightened public awareness about the need to preserve the environment. New wildlife reserves were established, as were national parks, sanctuaries for migrating birds, animal orphanages, petting zoos, and ecological reserves, which conserved plants, trees, and clean air and water. By the 1990s, the efforts of Joy and other naturalists had resulted in twenty-one national parks in the United States; six in France; twelve in Japan, North Korea, and South Korea; ten in Spain and Portugal; and fifty-four in Africa. In the United States, where approximately eighteen percent of the land, excluding military bases, remains in the hands of the government, four federal agencies help safeguard the country's flora and fauna: the U.S. Forest Service, the Fish and Wildlife Service, the Bureau of Land Management, and the National Park Service.

With their new consciousness about the environment, politicians have passed laws to protect endangered species. Partly due to the impact of Joy's work, it is possible that Japan won't lose its endangered short-tailed albatrosses, or Hawaii its monk seals, or Brazil its golden-lion tamarin monkeys, or California its red-legged frogs. Cheetahs may finally flourish in Africa, wolves might be welcome again in U.S. national parks, and whales might multiply once more in the great oceans.

Joy and renowned naturalists like Rachel Carson (who fought to ban pesticides), Jacques Cousteau (an underwater explorer), and Dian Fosse and Jane Goodall (both of whom studied gorillas and chimpanzees) brought the world's attention to the sacredness of life on earth. The tenacity of these naturalists gave rise to the popular Green movements, which endeavor to support both the environment and animal rights. In 1996, tens of thousands of animal activists gathered in Washington, D.C., for World Animal Awareness Week, marching to the White House to expose the injustice that threatens millions of animals.

Even while hunger, poverty, illiteracy, mass slaughter, and disease persist in Africa, democracy and economic opportunity from foreign investments have grown. And while Kenya's national parks and reserves experience difficulties meeting costs, new funds are being raised; tourists, for example, are charged a fee to view wildlife in the Masai Mara National Reserve, and must pay to join safaris.

In the year after Joy's death, her trust in England turned Elsamere into the Elsamere Conservation Center and opened it to the public. Signs of Joy are ever present: her easel, where she so often sketched and painted; her photos and carvings on walls and shelves; her library of books. She seems about to arrive from the bush, perhaps with an abandoned monkey in tow, or an injured squirrel. Hanging from a hook, as if she just left it, is the high, broad-brimmed straw hat she bought in Niger for a safari across the Sahara Desert.

George, even more silent without Joy, turned white-haired and gaunt at Kora. He wrote two books of his own (*Bwana Game* and *My Pride and Joy*), but in August 1989, in his eighty-fourth year, he tried to save a German woman from Somali bandits and was shot in the back and killed. He was buried at Kora beside his brother Terence's grave, his funeral attended by friends such as Ken Smith, who was with him when he'd found Elsa, and

Bill Travers and Virginia McKenna. Newspaper obituaries commented that both Joy and George Adamson had died in Kenya nearly ten years apart, not from a wild animal's teeth or claws, but from attacks by human beings with their civilized "tools."

Together, Joy and George created what Jane Goodall described in 1992 as a "special place in history" and a "major accomplishment for science." For Joy, the call of the wild had always been a call to recognize that the commonality existing between all life-forms is far stronger than any differences.

Joy knew this commonality when she saw a flower turn toward the sun or a fish hide from its attackers. She knew it when Pati, the rock hyrax who'd become a nanny to three lion cubs, ground her teeth in happiness. She saw it when an elephant grieved over its dead brother or Pippa dragged herself home on a broken leg. And she believed it most with Elsa—in Elsa's moments of love and delight, sadness and pain, protectiveness and pride. Elsa had so often been the teacher, not the student, in Joy's domain. And what Joy had learned from her lion, and from the rich beauties and inevitable sufferings of life in Africa, was to yield to the cycles and colors of nature, to embark not just on a physical adventure but on a spiritual safari that would never really end.

ℬIBLIOGRAPHY

Adamson, George. *Bwana Game*. London: Collins Harvill, 1968.

———. *My Pride and Joy*. London: Collins Harvill, 1986.

Adamson, Joy. *Born Free: A Lioness of Two Worlds*. New York: Pantheon Books, 1960.

———. *Elsa and Her Cubs*. New York: Harcourt, Brace & World, 1965.

———. *Elsa: The True Story of a Lion*. New York: Pantheon Books, 1961.

———. *Forever Free*. New York: Harcourt, Brace & World, 1962.

———. *Friends from the Forest*. New York: Harcourt Brace Jovanovich, 1981.

———. *Joy Adamson's Africa*. New York: Harcourt Brace Jovanovich, 1972.

———. *Living Free*. New York: Harcourt, Brace & World, 1961.

———. *The Peoples of Kenya*. New York: Harcourt, Brace & World, 1967.

———. *Pippa's Challenge*. New York: Harcourt Brace Jovanovich, 1972.

———. *Pippa, the Cheetah and Her Cubs*. New York: Harcourt Brace Jovanovich, 1972.

———. *Queen of Shaba: The Story of an African Leopard*. New York and London: Harcourt Brace Jovanovich, 1980.

———. *The Searching Spirit: Joy Adamson's Autobiography*. New York and London: Harcourt Brace Jovanovich, 1978.

———. *The Spotted Sphinx*. New York: Harcourt, Brace & World, 1969.

Burton, Robert, ed. *Nature's Last Strongholds*. New York: Oxford University Press, 1991.

Croke, Vicki. *The Modern Ark: The History of Zoos: Past, Present and Future*. New York: Charles Scribner's Sons, 1997.

Dyer, Anthony. *Classic African Animals: The Big Five*. New York: Winchester Press, 1973.

Heller, P. J. "A Walk on the Wild Side." Chicago: *Chicago Tribune*, Sunday, May 25, 1997, section 13.

House, Adrian. *The Great Safari: The Lives of George and Joy Adamson, Famous for Born Free*. New York: William Morrow and Company, 1993.

New York Times News Service. "Kenya Promotes 'Conservation for Profit' to Save Wildlife." Chicago: *Chicago Tribune*, Friday, March 15, 1996, section 1.

Schreuder, Cindy. "Kenya's Game Plan: Find Ways to Make Wildlife Pay." Chicago: *Chicago Tribune,* Monday, October 9, 1995, section 1.

$\mathcal{I}$NDEX